REPLACING YOUR BOAT'S
ELECTRICAL SYSTEM

ADLARD
COLES
MANUAL

REPLACING YOUR BOAT'S
ELECTRICAL SYSTEM

MIKE WESTIN

ADLARD COLES NAUTICAL

BLOOMSBURY

LONDON · NEW DELHI · NEW YORK · SYDNEY

Published by Adlard Coles Nautical
an imprint of Bloomsbury Publishing Plc
50 Bedford Square, London WC1B 3DP
www.adlardcoles.com

Copyright © Michael Westin 2012
First published in Sweden by Norstedts
Published in the UK in 2013 by Adlard Coles Nautical

10 9 8 7 6

ISBN 978-1-4081-3293-7
ePDF 978-1-4081-5929-3
e-Pub 978-1-4081-5930-9

A CIP catalogue record for this book is available from the
British Library.

This book is produced using paper that is made from
wood grown in managed, sustainable forests. It is natural,
renewable and recyclable. The logging and manufacturing
processes conform to the environmental regulations of the
country of origin.

Translation: Marie Allen
Design by James Watson
Page layout by Susan McIntyre
Typeset in 9.75 on 12pt URWGrotesk
Printed and bound in India by Replika Press Pvt. Ltd.

Note: While all reasonable care has been taken in
the publication of this book, the publisher takes no
responsibility for the use of the methods or products
described in this book.

The author wishes to thank the following contributors:
Jonas Arvidsson, Herman Beijerbergen, Per Hjelm, Torulf
Holmström, Anders Jangö, Lars Lundbladh, Bengt Odelfors,
Kim Rask, Jan-G Westin and many more

>> # CONTENTS

>> INTRODUCTION: PRACTICAL RATHER THAN THEORETICAL ...

This aim of this book is to provide a highly practical, step-by-step approach to upgrading your boat's old electrical system – but first of all, I would like to say that I am no expert in 12 V DC electrics in boats.

A couple of years ago I started upgrading my own boat. As a novice, my approach was to listen to advice, but I didn't want to read and understand all the theory behind it – I just wanted to fix my boat's electrical system without having to be an engineer or a rocket scientist...

If you want to learn all about the theory of electricity, it's quite easy. There are many weighty tomes as well as numerous articles on the Peukert coefficient, detailed CE regulation, or what amperes, ohms and volts are all about. I would definitely recommend reading a couple of these books if you really want to find out about upgrading your onboard electrical system on a more theoretical level before starting your project.

If, on the other hand, you only want to upgrade your boat without having to wade through a sea of theory, I'll be explaining the somewhat simplified practical aspects of upgrading your electrical system in this book.

It won't be entirely without theory and will include some simple mathematical calculations. But I'll try to keep this aspect to the bare minimum – how to calculate the required size of the battery bank and how to decide the optimal diameter for your cables are among the tasks where a pocket calculator may come in handy among the tasks where some calculations will have to be done.

In this book we'll look at assessing when it's time to change the electrical system and how to calculate the capacity of the new system. You will also learn how to choose the right batteries, get the best charge, create neat wiring, install solar panels/wind power, and much more – all in a simple, step-by step approach.

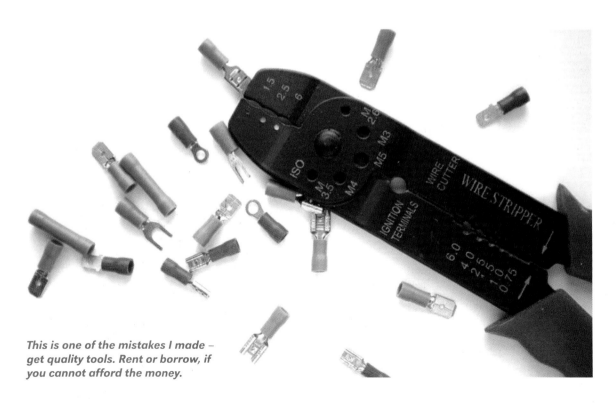

This is one of the mistakes I made – get quality tools. Rent or borrow, if you cannot afford the money.

DO YOUR RESEARCH

As usual for me, I started my own research at the boat shows, where I cross-examined the experts who know all there is to know about boat electrics.

My extended research also included the Internet, where there are many good sources of information. But I couldn't find one website that contained all the necessary information, and even on the Internet there are widely differing views about how things should be assembled. As an almost complete beginner, that only made me even more confused.

I browsed through several books about electrical systems for boats, but I'm less interested in the theory behind it all than in how to go about it in practice – and unfortunately I didn't find much information about that. It was this lack of practical information that prompted my decision to replace the electrical system myself, keeping DIY notes on the progress of the project, rather than hand the job over to a specialist (and by doing it myself, I saved hundreds of pounds/dollars).

And if I can do it – I'm sure you can, too!

So, even if I have simplified some projects and made generalizations in the text, the aim is to help enable you to replace the electrics in your boat without encountering any major problems. When you are really unsure how to proceed, ask an expert – most are quite happy to help, especially if you buy equipment from them.

CONFLICTING ADVICE...

Throughout the installations, while I was on my learning curve, I received a lot of advice from many directions, but it rarely meant the same thing.

However, as I am somewhat stubborn by nature, I kept asking different people until I received an answer I felt satisfied with. But I do think it is hard to obtain good information on practical solutions – what to buy, what diameter the cables should be or how to actually wire the alternator...

There were times of frustration because of problems with tracking down the right information, but as I learnt more, the 'Aha!' moments became more frequent.

I hope I will manage to convey some of these 'Aha!' moments in the book, and that you will be able to add my experiences to those of other people and make up your own mind on how to carry out your upgrading project.

About Mike Westin

Mike is a boating journalist cruising on his yacht *Roobarb* part time. 2003 he started a practical boating magazine that became extremely popular, but is now the editor-in-chief of a cruising magazine to be able to combine work with sailing.

His background is as a sailing instructor, tall ship first mate, Swedish Navy and did a 1.5 year cruise in his last boat across the Pacific.

Back in Stockholm, Mike is also a coxswain with the local Life boat, a Port Officer for the Ocean Cruising Club and he is also currently building an 8-metre 'spirit of tradition' yacht with both an electric motor and gaff rig.

ABOUT THE PROJECT BOAT, A VANCOUVER 27

Americans call this type of small, long-distance boat a 'pocket cruiser', and it was in North America that Rob Harris designed the Vancouver 27 in the late 1960s for a couple planning to cross the South Pacific from Canada to New Zealand. The boat type proved more than up to the task, and series production commenced a few years later. In total 250 of the type 27 were built, both in Canada and in England. A minor modification was made to the design in 1983, and about 60 of the Vancouver 28 were then produced and are still being built to order.

The project boat *Roobarb* was built from a kit in 1977, and I purchased it 25 years later to use as a practical platform for the articles in the Swedish boating magazine I set up in 2003.

This boat type is not common in Scandinavia, but *Roobarb* displays most of the faults and flaws of 1970s boats and so is a very suitable candidate for a renovation and improvement project – from a new grooved teak deck to building a brand new galley. The eventual goal was to sail the boat long-distance, to show what you can do even on a limited budget.

1. *Security; CE-approved LED mast top navigation + anchor light.*

Foredeck flood light and orange glow panel in main sail and orange + reflective tape in mast top for better visibility on the ocean.

2. *Running rigging; changed from wire to rope halyards. New standing rigging and correct adjustment of the rig.*

New bigger self-tailing winches and old ones repositioned for better use on cabintop for halyards. Roller reefing both on staysail with newly developed stainless steel roller and on genoa with off the shelf roller.

Crosstree refurbishment with new end fittings and chafe padding. Home made lazy jacks and sail cover.

3. *Raised main sheet track on gantry to make room for bimini. Home made spray hood + sunroof, waterproof cushions in cockpit.*

4. *Foldable tiller with brackets for wind vane and autopilot.*

Extra window into cockpit for large plotter/PC.

Wind generator pole and solar panels brackets on gantry to generate power when anchored.

5. *New stronger 25 bhp three-cylinder diesel engine with all systems upgraded to new specification to comply with coming stricter environment legislation.*

6. *Repainted hull with 2-part polyurethane paint and brush + new shine of gelcoat with wet sanding 2000/4000 grade paper.*

7. *Recaulked teak deck and how-to service teak for longer life.*

8. *Bowsprit for headsail + cruising chute.*

Anchor windlass with chain stop and chain-well moved back for chain to be stored low in forepeak, below waterline.

9. *Interior improvements: Galley rebuilt with new countertop of Corian.*

Spring mattresses in bunks.

Windows and foredeck hatch changed into both off-the-shelf and robust home constructions of 316 stainless steel and 10 mm extra reinforced polycarbonate (Lexan).

Paint and construction of seating + teak veneering of plywood floorboards

About the Vancouver 27

Length: *8.23 m (27 ft)*

LWL: *6.99 m (23 ft)*

Beam: *2.66 m (8.75 ft)*

Draught: *1.30 m (4.25 ft)*

Displacement: *approx. 4.1 metric tonnes (just over 5 loaded)*

In the hull: *1.6 tonnes lead*

Sail area: *35.2 m² (378 sq ft)*

Engine: *Vetus M3.09 25 hp*

Diesel: *245 l (54 gal)*

Water: *approx. 100 l (22 gal)*

Builders: *Northshore/kit*

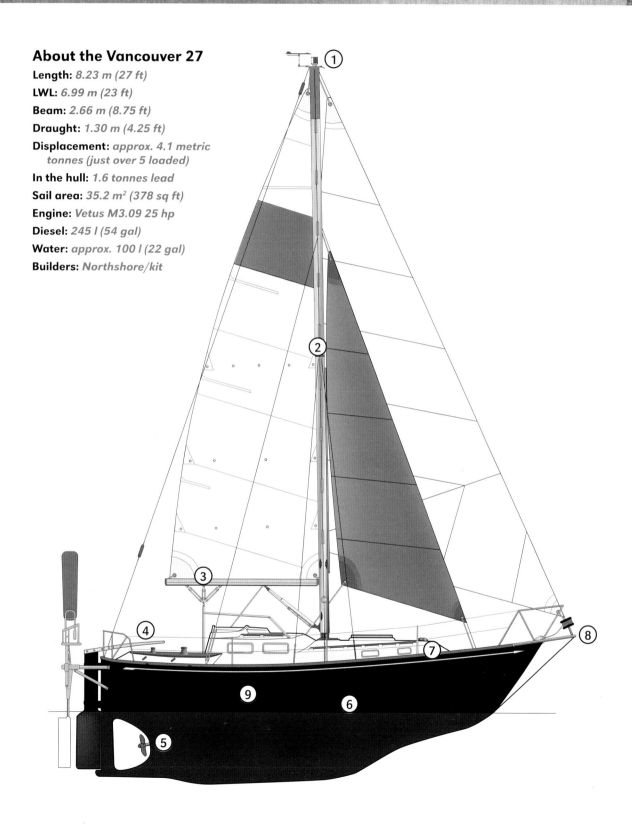

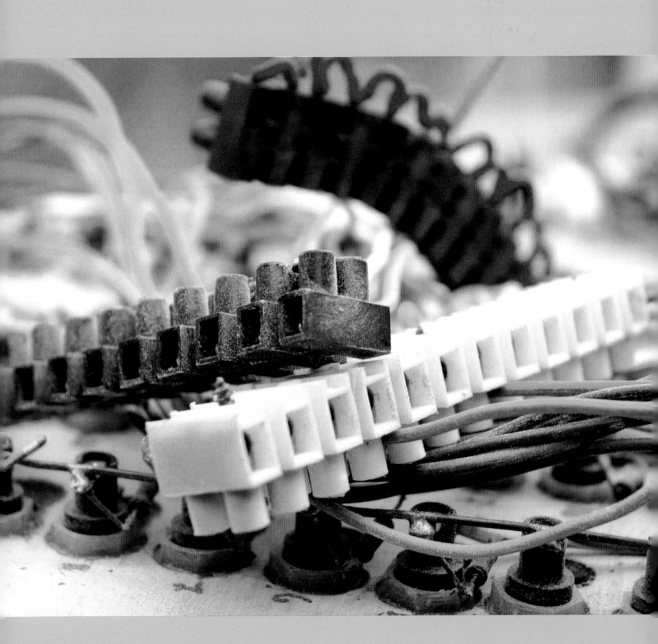

01
WHEN DOES A SYSTEM NEED UPGRADING?

>> CHECKING THE OLD

The first sign of trouble with the electrical system was that I noticed the batteries were losing power more quickly than before, and that I had to fiddle with the fuses several times each season to remove oxidation. There were strange power drops, making the lights flicker.

I did a few random checks in the boat and stripped some electrical wiring to see if there was any oxidation (often in the form of a green or black coating on the copper wires). You often find this on boat wiring, and if it is in evidence in several places along the cable then it has probably come to the end of its life and you're going to have to bite the bullet and replace it, especially in those high-current circuits such as the anchor windlass or refrigerator. The knock-on effect can be a reduction in current, which means that equipment won't work as it should.

My investigation revealed not only oxidized cables, but also that the first owner had added a lot of electrical equipment, thus creating a confused tangle of wires. There were also electrical components and cables that looked as if they were left over from renovating a house, such as old twist-on wire connectors, green-yellow earth cables and so on. I decided the easiest course of action would be to strip it all out and start again.

The state of the existing system was appalling – the cables were corroded, and the installation was a mess.

Upgrading an electrical system can be expensive, typically between £800 and £2,500, or more if you install a lot of new components. If you can keep some of the old components you'll save quite a bit of money. But if your system has been around for the past 15, 20 or maybe even 30 years, it doesn't pay to hang on to much of it. Some of the smaller electrical items can stay, if they're still in good working order.

Screw top connectors for joining cables were used throughout the old system.

The battery cables were barely fastened to the quick-release battery terminals. I could pull them loose easily by hand.

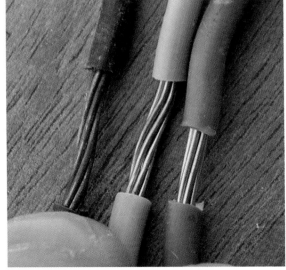

The colour coding was non-existent, and the installation process had clearly been a haphazard affair!

The best way to check to old cables is to peel off a section of the cover. Black or green copper is not a good sign!

The old battery isolator had some oxidised surfaces, and needed replacement as well.

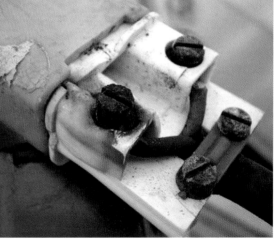

I discovered that the 240 V intake plug had at some point been short circuited – could have caused a nasty accident. The owners at the time must have been extremely lucky that a fire didn't break out as a result.

>> INITIAL PLANNING

The first thing I did was to make a rough diagram of the functions I wanted to include in the new system. I soon realized that the better the planning, the better the installations would be later – spending time designing the project and getting advice from a professional can cut some hassle later on.

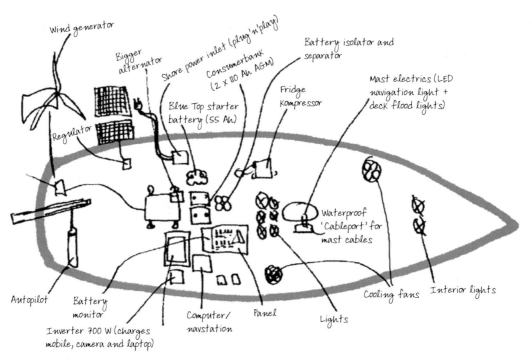

There were extensions and additions in the old system that had been there for decades. Although there was some labelling, I thought it would be easier for me, as the person who would be carrying out any repairs in the future, to start from the beginning and renew everything. A positive side effect of this was learning about the entire electrical system at the same time as I was installing it.

This is what I wanted:

- A 230-volt shore power system with a circuit breaker, a galvanic isolator and a waterproof socket for the cable.
- A multi-step charger from a reputable manufacturer to take the best possible care of the batteries.
- A larger alternator than the one that came originally with the new engine (I'll keep the old one in reserve for emergencies).

- A well laid-out distribution panel with automatic fuses to distribute the power, carried along good quality tin-plated stranded wires to the appliances.

To calculate how much battery capacity was needed, I carefully worked out how I used power over an average day. In fact, I split my calculations into two periods, because there is a difference in consumption between when I am sailing and when I am at anchor for a couple of days.

The largest power users are the compressor for the refrigerator, the computer/plotter and the cabin and navigation lights.

Another heavy power consumer is the *autopilot*, but that will be used mainly when I'm under engine and the power consumption is of less importance.

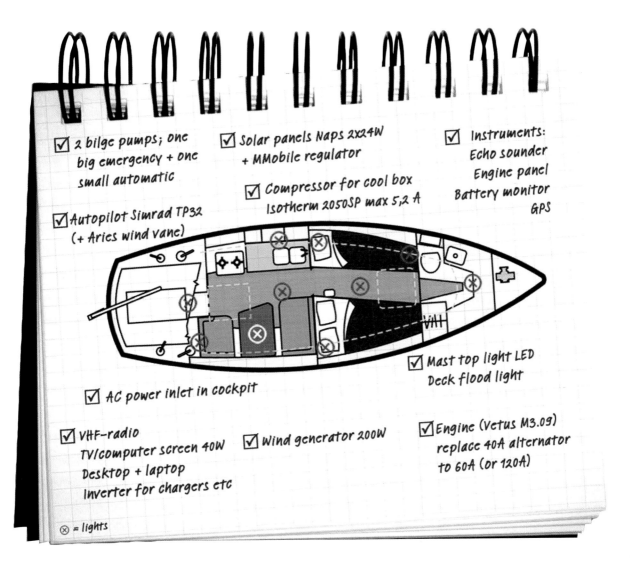

☑ 2 bilge pumps; one big emergency + one small automatic

☑ Autopilot Simrad TP32 (+ Aries wind vane)

☑ Solar panels Naps 2x24W + MMobile regulator

☑ Compressor for cool box Isotherm 2050SP max 5,2 A

☑ Instruments: Echo sounder Engine panel Battery monitor GPS

☑ Mast top light LED Deck flood light

☑ AC power inlet in cockpit

☑ VHF-radio TV/computer screen 40W Desktop + laptop Inverter for chargers etc

☑ Wind generator 200W

☑ Engine (Vetus M3.09) replace 40A alternator to 60A (or 120A)

⊗ = lights

Initially, I did lots of sketches (above and left) on how best to place all the electrical equipment I needed on my rather small boat. The drawings really helped me to understand how it would fit in, and where the cables would run. To make a functional plan was trickier, though, especially since this was the first project of this kind I'd ever undertaken. A couple of hours' consultancy from an experienced boat electrician would have been money well spent to help the project get off the ground. On the next page is the list of the equipment I planned to install.

TYPICAL POWER CONSUMPTIONS

This can be a useful calculation to make before deciding the size the domestic bank should be.

Apart from the consumers mentioned here, I have to consider the inverter – what it will draw depends, of course, on what you plug into it, but normally it is only for a short time.

An example is to boil some water in a kettle. A typical consumption is 2200 W at 220 V = 10 A, but only for 4–5 minutes. My small inverter, at 300 W, would not be able to handle this load – I only use it to charge mobile phones and the computer. In the calculation I used maximum power just to get a figure.

There is a small consumption (0.5–1.5 A) from an inverter whenever it is on, which can drain the house battery bank if left for a week or two, so make sure there is an 'off' switch. Read more on inverters in chapter 8.

Right: According to the specs, a Lopolight mast head nav light with light-emitting diodes draws around 4.9 watts (4.9 W divided by 12.75 V = 0.38 A) – about 10 h x 0.38 A = 3.8 Ah during a night sail, compared with 25 W divided by 12.75 V = 2 A x 10 h = 20 Ah for the normal 25-watt bulb in the tricolour light I replaced. That's a 500 per cent difference in power consumption for a typical night sail.

A wind generator is one excellent way to keep your battery banks topped up without having to run the engine or find a marina.

A bilge pump can be a big drain of DC current since it will be turned on even when you are not aboard, to take care of minor leaks that may occur. If a small but persistent leak occurs, even a small pump may drain the batteries very fast and sink the boat.

A small Whale 500 (flow rate of 925 litres/244 US gals per hour at 2-metre lift) draws 2.5 A.

The new system will initially consist of these components:

- Refrigerator: Isotherm 2050SP with water cooling (0.6–2.5 A)
- Autopilot: Simrad TP32 (average 0.5 A)
- Navigation lights: Lopolight LED tricolour with anchor light (4.9/2.1 A)
- Computer + stand-alone screen (plotter + work + entertainment) (approximately 3–3.5 A)
- Radio: fixed VHF + antenna in the mast
- 230-volt inverter: 350 W for mobile phone chargers (too small for kettle)
- Shore power plug-and-play system, intake and distribution
- Batteries: Leoch (approximately 2 x 100 Ah for house bank)
- Battery charger x 2 (house + start)
- Start battery: SpiralCell blue top (55 Ah)
- Battery monitor: Masterlink BTM-1
- Deck lighting (500 W)
- Motor panel (supplied with the engine)
- Wind generator: Air Breeze
- Solar panels: Naps (2 x 24 W)
- Instruments, echo sounder etc
- GPS + external antenna
- Bilge pumps (2 x electric, 1 x automatic)
- 12-volt outlets at navigation station + cockpit for search light, charger, etc
- Lighting: LEDs and halogen (total approximately 20 lights in cabin and on deck)

On board Roobarb there's a manual windlass. An electrical windlass is very hungry for power but only for a very short while and mostly when the engine is running to take care of the extra load. A typical electrical windlass draws 500 W or almost 40 A. The The cable's cross sectional area needs to be large, or alternatively an extra bank of batteries can be placed next to the windlass.

The autopilot is not an electrical item used for long periods of time since I have an Aries wind wane for longer crossings. When I use the autopilot it's usually because I'm motoring in light winds or close to the coast where I need an accurate course. The Simrad TP32 manual states the average consumption as 0.5 A per hour: 0.5 A x 3 h = 1.5 Ah, for example. Used for 24 hours it will be 12 Ah.

The new Isotherm refrigerator has a stated efficiency rating of 2.5 A when the compressor is running, and since the compressor is not running continuously, the average consumption during 24 hours can be calculated to 0.6 A as per information from the manufacturer. (Power consumption at +6°C inside the refrigerator, ambient temperature +22°C and a 67-litre volume; 'normal insulation' = 50 mm thickness.)

My laptop (with 15" LCD screen), which has a couple of digital chart programmes, uses a maximum of 65 W (65 W divided by 12.75 V is approximately 5 A), according to the label underneath the power unit. The average consumption is approximately 3.5 A, depending on how long the hard drive is running and whether peripheries are connected (this is checked with the new battery meter). If I use the computer as a plotter for 6 hours a day, that will be 3.5 A x 6 h = 21 Ah. If used for 24 hours it will be as high as 84 Ah.

Lately I have used my iPad with two or three different chart-apps downloaded for navigation, and run it on its internal batteries, which theoretically last up to 10 hours according to Apple, but 6–8 hours seems more likely from my experience.

I charge the iPad whenever the engine is running through the inverter or we stay in a marina with shore power. An optional extra is to buy a 12-volt charger from Apple.

A bonus is that, if not touched for a couple of minutes, the iPad shuts down in energy-saving mode, but starts right up when needed.

A marine GPS with digital charts cannot do as many things as a computer, but is more power-efficient (and normally has a better screen in sunlight).

The stated consumption for a typical small (5") chart plotter, draws around 10 W. 10 W divided by 12.75 V = 0.8 A, and for a 6-hour period 0.8 A x 6 h = 4.8 Ah.

Over 24 hours, a chart plotter will consume just under 20 Ah, just a quarter of what the computer will consume in the same period.

FOCUS

ESTIMATING YOUR ELECTRICITY USAGE

Power consumption is measured in ampere hours (Ah). To find your electrical system's power requirements, and hence specify the capacity of battery bank(s) you will need, divide power consumption (W) of each piece of electrical equipment by the system voltage (V) to find its current drain in amperes (A). You then multiply by the number of hours you expect to use the equipment to find its power requirement in ampere hours (Ah).

A fully charged wet cell battery is roughly 13 volts (but can be 14 volts or more after being charged) and a battery is discharged at 12 volts. Thus the average voltage of a normal lead acid battery is 12.75 volts, so I have used this throughout my calculations.

Spreadsheet – Roobarb's DC load calculation						
			Hours	Total Ah	Hours	Total Ah
Consumer	Watt	Ampere	At Anchor	At Anchor	Sailing	Sailing
Navigation lights	4.90	0.38	0.00	0.00	10.00	3.80
Cabin lights		1.57	4.00	5.41	3.00	4.71
Anchor light	2.10	0.16	10.00	1.60	0.00	0.00
Fridge		0.60	24.00	14.40	24.00	14.40
Plotter/computer		3.50	3.00	9.42	6.00	18.84
Autopilot		0.50	0.00	0.00	3.00	1.50
Inverter	350.00	27.45	0.10	2.75	0.00	0.00
Total				33.58		43.25

Your own 12 Volts budget						
			Hours	Total	Hours	Total Ah
Consumer	Watt	Ampere	At Anchor	At Anchor	Sailing	Sailing
Total						
Average voltage in the system = 12.75 V						

THE 30 PER CENT LIMIT

When you specify your electrical system, don't make it either too small or too large (and thus unnecessarily expensive). However, bear in mind that your power requirements will vary and you want to make sure you can cope with most situations without adding to the costs and complexities involved.

According to the usage calculation in my spreadsheet (see page 19), I would need approximately 45 ampere hours (Ah) over a 24-hour period when sailing and around 34 Ah when lying at anchor.

I planned never to draw more than about 30 per cent of the capacity from a battery bank as this shortens the life expectancy of the batteries – in my case, 30 per cent equals around 60 Ah (out of the 200 Ah bank) before I would need to charge.

That is probably not enough power to cover every eventuality, or even a few days at the same anchorage, but I would partly rely on the solar panels and the wind generator to provide the extra energy needed if I didn't want to either start the engine every day or head for a marina where I could fully recharge the batteries from shore power.

An advanced battery meter would keep track of the onboard power use and let me know when I needed to charge.

FOCUS

INTERVIEW WITH BOAT ELECTRICS EXPERT BENGT ODELFORS

What usually goes wrong in an old electrical system?

A common problem is that old fuse boxes with glass or automotive fuses are corroded.

Power drops are also common, due to a poor battery switches connection, oxidized cable shoes, or terminal blocks in the charging and starter circuits, for example. One construction error is an underrating in both the cross-sectional cable area and alternator capacity.

What components should a new system include and what parts of the old system can normally be reused?

I don't think anything can be saved and used again – there shouldn't be any weak links in a new wiring system. If you want to/must save something because of financial considerations, it would have to be cables and switches for lighting and small appliances that draw little current. However, you must install new thicker cabling for the refrigerator, heating and autopilot, as well as other larger and vital items, such as the bilge pump. Power drops in cables connected to these result in impaired performance and cost ampere hours.

In a 25-year-old boat the alternator, too, will be so worn out that it will need replacing, even if the original priority was to change it because it lacks the capacity to provide sufficient power for today's onboard needs.

If you have a diode bridge in your old electrical system then that should also be replaced - not because a diode wears out, but because it causes such a large power drop that in most cases charging will be greatly affected.

What are the most common difficulties for a DIY beginner?

Many people who want to replace the fuse holder or panel, for example, cut off or disconnect the cables without making a note of where they lead.

Another problem beginners can come up against is the capacity of the cables in relation to their length and power consumption. Many catalogues have a nomogram (a graphical calculating device) for this purpose.

What's the cost of rewiring an 8-metre semi-finished boat, for example?

That's hard to answer, but material costs naturally depend on the kind of quality you're aiming for. A basic kit costs around £250 and contains the components necessary for the charging and starter circuits, as well as cables. Added to that, of course, is a long list of components, such as fuse holders and distribution panels, trip switch panels, cables, etc. The total price could be around £1,200, and that could double if your alternator/regulator is also going to be replaced, especially if you want first-class equipment.

The starter motor of an old engine should also be replaced or reconditioned.

The project boat _Roobarb_ is going on a long-distance voyage, so the system must be as simple as possible, tolerate heat and salty damp air, and be able to be left unattended on land for long periods. What do you recommend?

Replace everything! Use tin-plated copper cables, get a new alternator and a new regulator to control the alternator's charging current in relation to the prevailing battery temperature, and which measures the current at the battery and not at the alternator.

Fit at least one solar panel to keep the batteries topped up when the boat is left unmanned – don't rely on a shoreside connection being available.

Grease all connections/cable shoes/terminal blocks and connectors with Vaseline so that the damp can't corrode the metal. As far as possible, use ring cable terminals, and flat pin connectors only when unavoidable.

Fit a good battery monitor, which could best be described as a computerized, ampere-hour counter for the battery banks. This instrument provides all sorts of important information about the battery, charging and discharging, and is definitely worth the reasonable cost involved.

There are, however, some instruments that aren't as good and should be avoided. And don't think a voltmeter can replace a battery monitor!

BENGT'S TOP 5 TIPS

1. Replace all circuits that draw a lot of current.

2. Use thick enough cable so that the power drop does not exceed 3 per cent.

3. Ensure you have several charging sources, not just the engine.

4. Understand that the electrical system is one of the boat's most important functions. If it goes wrong it can cause problems with everything else. For complete control, connect a battery monitor.

5. If you're not used to working with electrics it's a good idea to let an electrician do the job. You can fit some of the components on his instructions.

02

TOOLS AND EQUIPMENT

>> FINDING THE RIGHT GEAR

The actual sourcing of good quality installation material turned out to be the most difficult part of the project, maybe together with planning where to put everything in a small boat.

It helps tremendously to know where to source the material, otherwise it is a chore to try to find anything off the web – you really need to know exactly what you are looking for.

Most chandlers were unfortunately not very helpful and would normally only stock the cheapest available material. I guess that is what we customers are asking for, if we are not given better advice.

It is considerably easier to order online from Maplin or similar, for example, but in my opinion the products are not of a consistent (high) quality. It is possible to order good-quality installation materials through boat electrics specialists like Merlin and Marathon, and this is how I ended up getting most of what I needed. These companies provide good advice and information, which can be worth paying extra for.

A (very) few chandlers do have quality products on the shelves, and it is of course easier if you can check out the goods before buying! Or visit the boat shows to check out what is available – also a good place where you can ask all the tricky questions.

The fact boxes about installation materials are the result of research that cost me many miles in the car...

Right: Some chandlers now offer quality cable and the possibility to crimp the lugs in the shop - excellent service!

CRIMPERS AND CUTTERS

Most failure is to be found in wiring connections. Double-crimp ratchet tools use gearing to compress the terminal, and the ratchet does not release until the cable clip is correctly crimped. This type of tool costs approximately £25 and is suitable for red, blue and yellow cable clips.

Crimping

It is important to crimp the cable clips properly. For the larger conduit clips, heavy pliers are required, which can be hired; alternatively, the crimping can be done at a boat equipment store. For smaller cable dimensions you need good cable clip pliers (see page 43).

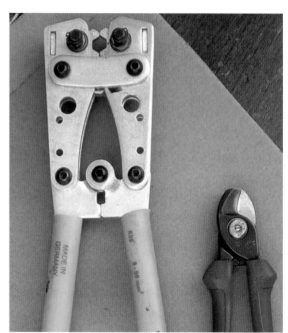

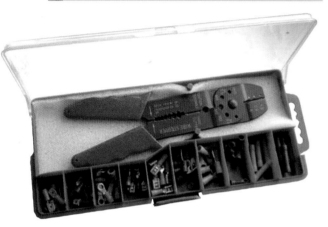

Above: This kit cost almost £7.50 from the chandler, while I found exactly the same box for £1.20 at a discount store. Neither of them is worth the money – my best advice is to buy, rent or borrow proper equipment.

Right, top: This hexagonal crimping tool (on left) crimps cables up to 120 mm². The technique takes a little practice, as you need to hold the two cheeks of the tool, the lug and the stiff cable at the same time. If you support one of the cheeks against a firm base, it is somewhat easier. The pliers cost around £200, but they can be hired. They are sold by good chandlers, but are more often to be found in specialist shops. Klauke is one make.

There is a different type of crimper that you use with a sledgehammer or vice, but they are not as easy to use as the big pliers, while admittedly cheaper to buy.

Above: Parrot beak cable cutters easily cut through a 35 mm² cable with a clean result. They are also handy for stripping the rubber coating from heavy-duty cables. These cutters from Knipex cost around £25.

Right: Double-crimp ratchet tools create a perfect crimp.

TERMINALS

Primarily use ring terminals, as they will not fall off. The colours of the terminal indicate the cable diameter they are intended for. Crimp with a crimper with release block for a perfect result. Buy quality terminals for use in boats.

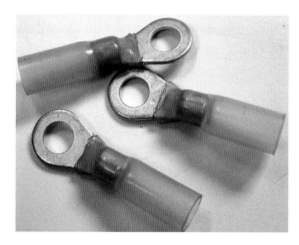

Heat shrink butt connectors will extend a cable. The adhesive offers a resistant protection to salt water and oil. Price from £4 for 10

Terminals with adhesive-lined heat shrink butt connectors are the best connection for water- and corrosion-proofing. Pricier than the standard variety, but withstand the moist salt environment in boats much better. Cost from £3 for 10.

For chunky battery cable you use tin-plated copper lugs crimped with special hexagonal pliers to create gas-proof crimping (or soldering) to the copper cable. The folded metal lug is not recommended in boats. Costs around £1 each.

CABLE TIES

 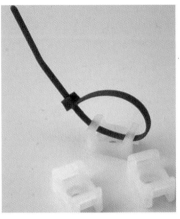 

The cable ties makes it easy to fasten cables in most places. Screwed down tie holder better than adhesive-backed ones.

Adhesive-backed plastic cable tie holders that stick on surfaces where you prefer not to use screws. Cost about £6 for 10.

Perfect for keeping cables together when they are not in a conduit, these can be used for many purposes on board.

All cables should be securely fastened every foot/30 centimetres.

Above right: These cable clamps have stainless steel screws and come in four sizes for different-sized cables. Cost about £4 for 10 (with A4 screw).
This type is the one we used the most – very simple and versatile when used with a stainless steel screw. Cost about £5 for 100 (with nail).

Right: A sturdy stainless fastener for the coarser battery cables is advisable. The thicker cables can be quite heavy.

FUSES

Domestic automatic fuses (circuit breakers) are cost effective, but unfortunately rather bulky. They come in many sizes, but normally 10, 16 and 25 ampere are required for a boat.

Strangely enough domestic AC automatic fuses work fine in a DC environment. Price from £3.

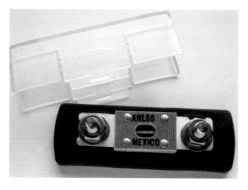

For fusing battery cables, a high amperage fuse should be used on both the negative and positive side. Amperage from 50 to 750 A. Place in a holder with a cover to protect from melted metal in a short-circuit. Price from £20.

This type of older glass fuse is common in a European standard (which is easy to find over here) but also in a US standard. The fuseholder is normally the weakest point of this type.

Older type of automotive fuses are prone to oxidation and the newer blade type are a better choice.

Above: A one-piece fuse holder for blade fuses. A compact unit is perfect for a smaller yacht and will keep everything in good order. Price from £ 40.

Newer blade type of automotive fuses are economical, can be found almost everywhere and take up little space. Up to 80 A.

MISCELLANEOUS

All cables should have a label describing what they are in clear text or with a code number. These have a plastic label for use with a permanent marker.

Attach the label to the cable with a cable tie. Price £5 for 10

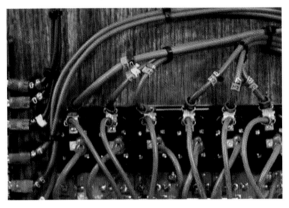

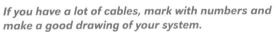

If you have a lot of cables, mark with numbers and make a good drawing of your system.

A dry cell battery-driven label maker makes a quick job of marking your cables. Choose a plastic tape with good glue and water-resistant qualities. Price from £20.

Heat shrink tubing in the colours black and red indicate whether there is positive or negative voltage in the battery cables. It can also be sealed with Vaseline to improve water resistance around the corrosion-prone ends of the cable. Price from £2 for 1 metre.

All cables should be pulled through PVC pipes or flexible split conduit tubing to protect against chafe.

Protect all connections and terminals with Vaseline – it does not dry out and provides permanent protection against corrosion by excluding oxygen.

CONNECTORS

A powerpost cable connector allows distribution directly from the busbar and battery to users like an automatic bilge pump. Price from £20

Right: The 'chocolate block' electrical connector comes in two varieties, neither of which is really suitable for use in a damp corrosive environment. With the simpler version, a screw goes directly into the cable, while in the other the screw goes into an indirect bearing that compresses the strands rather than divides them. From £1.

Left: Twist-on wire connectors are designed for use in houses, not boats. These are what I found everywhere in Roobarb on corroded wire ends. Waterproof varieties exist, but are still not a good choice. Approx £12 for 100.

Right: A modern version of the block is the barrier terminal busbar where the cables connect. It comes in many sizes and should be tin-plated brass for protection against corrosion. Price from £3 for 2 connections.

≫ HOW TO USE A MULTIMETER

A multimeter can give you some useful information to help with your upgrading project. They are quite inexpensive, between £10 and £20. Get one with a digital display, rather than an analogue multimeter – the digital display version is easy to read, hard to break, and there are not too many buttons to cause confusion. The simpler the better...

The common uses of multimeters need only a broad understanding of electrical circuits so they can be operated by almost anyone.

Most multimeters can measure voltage (volt/V), current (ampere/A) continuity and resistance (ohm/Ω), which is what you will most likely need. Most multimeters also measure 240/110 V AC, which is potentially lethal if handled, and I suggest you do not fiddle with this if you are unsure how to do it. The 12 V DC, as in a boat or car, is a lot safer.

An easy start is to check the voltage in the system, and to check the battery. This is not a conclusive test to check the status, as the battery needs to have been 'in rest', i.e. not used for the last 24 hours. A fully charged battery should show 12.7–12.8 V (more when freshly charged) and 11.6 V when discharged. At 10.5 V the battery is more or less dead. To check a battery under load, to decide if it needs replacing, it is better to use a battery meter as described in chapter 4.

Hands on: One lead on each terminal of the battery will tell you the voltage. If there's a minus sign before the figure on the display, just switch the leads – red for the positive (+) side and black for the negative (-) side.

The black lead should always be plugged into the 'common' terminal (marked COM), and the red lead into the amperage jack (A) for measuring ampere, and the volt/ohm jack (VΩ) for everything else. Not all multimeters function in the same way – check the manual before using yours.

The limit of a cheap multimeter is normally the size of current in ampere it can measure – the maximum will be stated on the unit or can be seen through the numbers at the selecting switch. The current that runs through the starter battery and the starter, and the shore power charging current, can be very high and probably cannot be measured with the cheap meter, which will have a limit of 10 A. Trying to meter greater amperage may destroy the multimeter.

VOLTAGE

To check for voltage drops that can prevent a refrigerator or heater starting at all, you put the leads on the terminals of the equipment and read the meter. Then start the equipment and check if there's a voltage drop – the power needed at start-up is much higher than the given figure and is a common failure. Always start with the highest setting (say 20 V if in a 12 V system) and if the display shows 0.001 or similar turn to the next one down until you get a good readout.

CURRENT

Measuring current in ampere (A). If there is a third jack on the meter for a test lead, it is probably marked 10 A or 20 A – or 200 mA (0.2 A) if it's a really cheap multimeter. This is for measuring high current. It is risky, in my opinion, unless you understand well the workings of the meter and the circuit you are playing with. I would leave it alone. The cheap multimeter will probably not be capable of measuring charging current from a shore power charger or the starting current from the engine battery.

To check what amperage a component draws, you either need to replace a part of the positive cable and put the meter in series with the cable, or you can use a clamp meter – a meter that you just clamp onto the cable and it measures the magnetic field to establish the current going through the cable. This meter is somewhat more expensive, but can be useful to detect faults in your system.

To check current you need to put the multimeter in series with the circuit to test - here I used the battery to test the amperage of a filament bulb lamp (out of picture).

To check which cable went to the lamp, I used the multimeter to identify the circuit with the least resistance. In the same way, you can check whether a lightbulb works – if there's high resistance it's broken, if there's low resistance, it's not.

A clamp meter is very easy to use on board to check consumption on a cable. They can usually handle large currents of 400–600 A.

A clamp meter does not have to be very expensive – it does everything a normal multimeter does so you don't need to get two units.

RESISTANCE

Resistance measurement in ohm (Ω) is used to check if a device is broken – a fully functional device should show a very low number, whereas a broken one will have a high number, indicating high resistance.

To check a light bulb, first take it out, switch the probe to Ω and put the leads across the two contacts at the bottom of the bulb. The measurement should read 0.000 ohm if it is OK – that is, no resistance and a fully functional circuit. If it still doesn't light up you can probe the contact in the bulb fitting to check that the voltage is there. If not, check whether the fuse has blown.

CONTINUITY

Testing for continuity with a multimeter is virtually the same as testing for resistance. Continuity tests whether or not electricity can pass between two points in a circuit. It tests if a circuit is open or closed, i.e. functioning as a yes and no – there are no units on the display. First turn off the device or take it out or unplug it; no current should be on. Turn the dial to the Ω reading (sometimes with a sign indicating a sound).

When the leads are not touching anything, the multimeter display will indicate a reading of infinity (or may just state '1') when the circuit is open. An open circuit cannot conduct electricity.

When you touch the two probes together, the reading changes to zero and a signal may beep. A reading of zero indicates that the circuit is closed, or functioning. A closed circuit is said to have continuity.

To test a cable or fuse for corrosion – a common problem in older boats – touch the cable at the two ends and check for a beep or zero ohm. Many devices can be checked in the same way.

With the multimeter set for continuity you can check for faulty circuits or equipment.

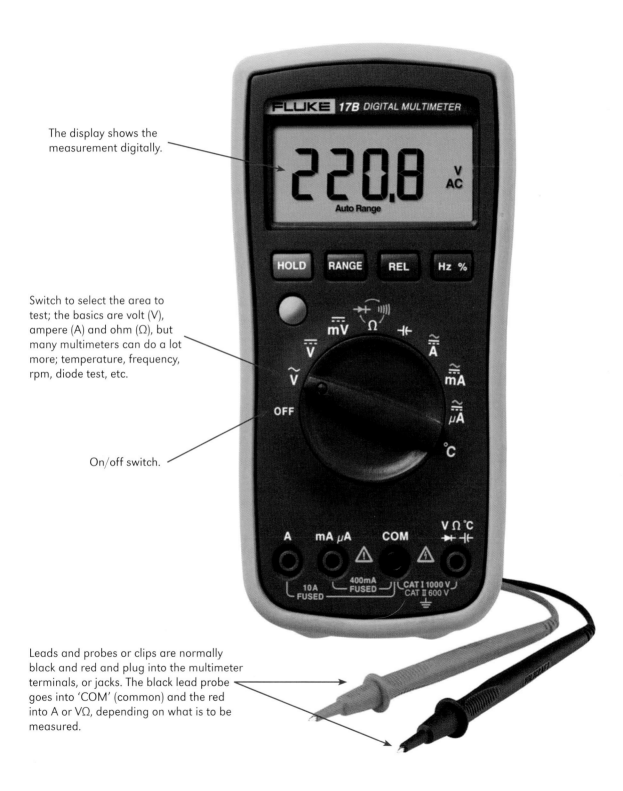

The display shows the measurement digitally.

Switch to select the area to test; the basics are volt (V), ampere (A) and ohm (Ω), but many multimeters can do a lot more; temperature, frequency, rpm, diode test, etc.

On/off switch.

Leads and probes or clips are normally black and red and plug into the multimeter terminals, or jacks. The black lead probe goes into 'COM' (common) and the red into A or VΩ, depending on what is to be measured.

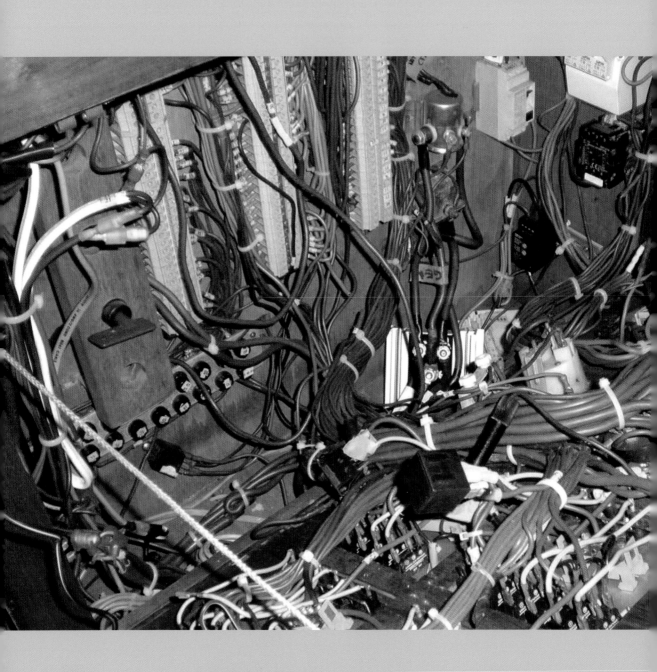

03

CABLES

GETTING THE REWIRING STARTED

After inspecting and chucking out almost all of the 30-year-old corroded electrical system on my project boat *Roobarb*, it was time to start replacing it with something more modern. I had made my calculation based on how much power I expected to use per day. Now it was time to begin the practical work.

It is best to start by planning the work properly – in the confined spaces of a yacht it is normally cramped and difficult to install things, so the better the planning, the better the end result. And planning is a phase where paying for professional help may prove to be money well spent, as it is not easy if you have never done anything similar before. If an expert points out what is needed and where best to place your new equipment, it will save you considerable time.

CABLES
New cables must be specified to avoid voltage drop as much as possible (that normally means less than 3 per cent) on the way to the consumer of power – the greater the cable diameter, the less is lost.

Of course, best of all would be to use heavy-duty cable everywhere. But chunky good-quality multi-strand tin-plated cable is very expensive and you need to try to determine the finest possible cable diameter you can use without causing an unacceptable loss of voltage.

In a few chandlers it is now possible to cut and crimp cables yourself, to your exact requirements. Measure carefully before you start cutting cables.

In recent years, there has been an increase in the

awareness and knowledge that cables of good quality and sufficient diameter boost the charge from the engine's alternator. These days it is somewhat easier to find good materials and also to get help to make new cables, find quality equipment, etc.

Make sure to make your installation safe, by installing fuses for the cables from the batteries for instance

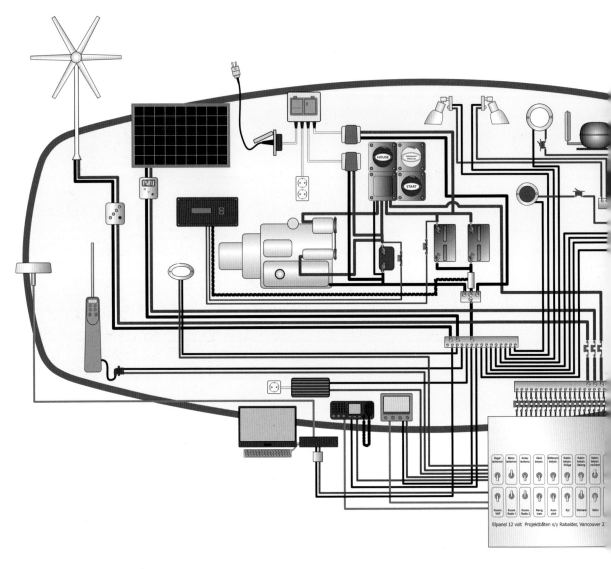

Elpanel 12 volt Projektbåten s/y Rabalder, Vancouver 2

The illustration shows a simplified plan of the electrical installation on Roobarb. There are batteries in two banks; 55 Ah in the starting battery and 200 Ah in the consumer bank. The capacity is a little on the low side, so I plan to use solar panels and a wind generator on the boat to add charging power. The alternator on the inboard engine is really the main source for charging the batteries, and I intend to let it run for a couple of hours every other day when I am holed up in a remote bay.

For those occasions when Roobarb is moored in a marina and I have access to shore power, there are two chargers on board, one for each of the battery banks.

The biggest power consumers will be the refrigerator compressor and the lights, because they are used for several hours every day. The computer and screen will also consume a great deal, depending on how much it will be on (average current drain is estimated to be around 3.5 A). It will be used for both navigation and my work – and for entertainment too, as it is nice to watch a DVD when it's raining outside.

On board there is also a small 350 W inverter, which converts 12 V to 230 V for various chargers – mobile phone, cameras, etc.

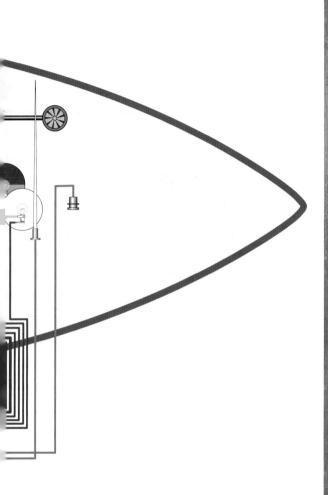

Calculating cable diameters

In the facts box on page 38, you can see how to calculate the dimensions of cables.

For *Roobarb* I used 35 mm^2 cable for everything between the batteries, engine and distribution busbars. After this point I reduced the dimensions of the wiring according to the current demands in each circuit.

Depending on the distance between the consumer and the distribution box, you can use different diameters for the cables. If you have a bow thruster or an electric anchor windlass you usually need very heavy-duty cables, as these are normally located at the bow. It's fairly common to have an extra battery bank at the bow for these consumers, thus reducing the length of cable runs.

The engine is located where it is designed to sit – under the companionway. Ideally, both the batteries and the distribution panel should be positioned as close to the engine as is practically possible.

My first idea for *Roobarb* was to put the roughly 90 kilos worth of batteries under the floorboards in the bilge, to keep the weight as low down in the boat as possible. Unfortunately space was tight, and I would have had to replace the batteries I'd already bought with a different size. Also the batteries are subject to water ingress in case of a leak and may be destroyed from a short curcuit. If the boat is sinking you will need your batteries to run the bilge pumps.

Instead, I chose the second-best place, with the batteries located a little higher and off centreline, but right between the engine and the distribution box. That way, the heavy-duty battery cables could be made as short as possible.

The standard colour code in Europe is black for the negative side (-) and red for the positive side (+).

Choose the correct cable diameter

We have discussed the importance of not using a cable that is too fine. If it is too heavy-duty it will be expensive, so there is always a delicate balance to find. A cable nomogram (right) can be a helpful tool, or you can calculate by using a formula whereby you strive never to have a loss of more than 3 per cent for important equipment.

Example 1: A newly installed refrigerator in *Roobarb*, which uses a maximum of 2.5 A, is located 4 metres from the control panel. That is 8 metres there and back, resulting in a cable area of about 1.5 mm² at a loss of 3 per cent (I chose a larger diameter of 2.5 mm², to be on the safe side).

Example 2: A 1500 W bow propeller (located at the bow, 4 metres from the panel (= 8 metres there and back) needs a cable of 95 mm² (cost around £30 per metre, about £240 in total).

The mathematical calculation is:

Length of cable (cm) x max effect (W) x 0.000075

gives 800 x 1500 x 0.000075 = 90 mm².

That is close to 95 mm² (4/0AWG), which is what you will find at the chandler.

A nomogram (a graphical calculating device) can be used as a guide to the required cable area.

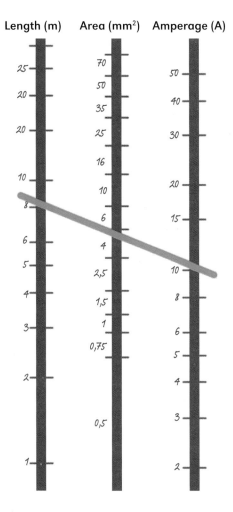

Length (m)	Area (mm²)	Amperage (A)

Above: To use the nomogram, you need to know the drain in A (or recalculate from the wattage) and the length of cable required to get there from the distribution panel and back. A 10 ampere radar unit is 4 metres from the distribution box (8 metres there and back) and gives a recommended cable diameter of 6 mm². Using a cable diameter one size up (i.e. 10 mm²) allows for initial start-up drain.

NOTE! When measuring the cable length in the boat, remember that the power will need to return to the fuse box and negative terminals, so you must double the value before you read the cable area in the nomogram.

Ready reckoner

For 10 metres of cables (i.e. in total, to equipment and back).

Current	Area
1 A (12 W)	0.75 mm²
2 A (24 W)	1.5 mm²
4 A (48 W)	2.5 mm²
6 A (72 W)	4.0 mm²
15 A (180 W)	8.0 mm²
30 A (360 W)	21.0 mm²

Right: For the cables, here is a selection of the most common diameters (tin-plated welding cable). If you have a cable of unknown diameter you can check against the image, since all the cables are illustrated at actual size.

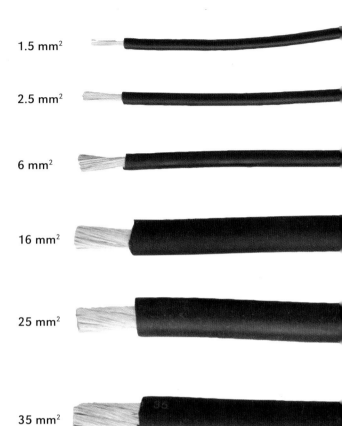

1.5 mm²

2.5 mm²

6 mm²

16 mm²

25 mm²

35 mm²

50 mm²

70 mm²

95 mm²

Label your cables and draw a plan of where everything goes. This will repay you tenfold a couple of years down the line, when you need to fix something in the system.

Also, make sure your labelling can withstand moisture and the occasional drip.

Cables should be protected when they run through the boat. The easiest way is to use the same type of conduits, PVC-piping, that are used in houses. Run cables of the same sort through each, more than one may be needed, and label them properly.

The drip protector. Sometimes it pays to make a loop in the cable so that water will not run along the cable into expensive equipment. Fasten the loop with cable ties. This will prevent water finding its way into the electrical equipment by running along the cable.

FOCUS

BUS SYSTEMS

Bus systems are now frequently used, and I definitely think they are the future for distributing electricity on bigger boats. But it will still be a few years before we leisure boat owners do the installation ourselves, even though I am sure this will eventually be the case.

The main benefits are the much smaller number of cables that need to be drawn in the boat. Instead there are intermediary units for power distribution, switching on/off, and other monitoring features controlled by a central computer device.

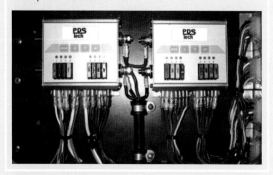

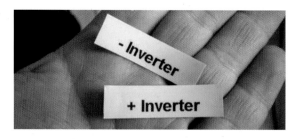

Above and below: If you do not have the space to spell out in text what each and every cable does, a system with numbers must be accompanied with a plan over the full system.

Above and below: Cables should be protected when they run through the boat.

Terminology on board

AWG (American wire gauge) Invented in 1857 by J.R. Brown and also known as the Brown & Sharp gauge, this is the system for cable gauging in the US. The lower the number, the greater the area.

6/0 AWG = 170.3 mm^2

5/0 AWG = 135.1 mm^2

4/0 AWG = 107.2 mm^2

3/0 AWG = 85.0 mm^2

2/0 AWG = 67.25 mm^2

0 AWG = 53.4 mm^2

1 AWG = 42.4 mm^2

2 AWG = 33.6 mm^2

4 AWG = 21.1 mm^2

6 AWG = 13.3 mm^2

8 AWG =   8.2 mm^2

10 AWG =   5.3 mm^2

12 AWG =   3.3 mm^2

13 AWG =   2.6 mm^2

14 AWG =   2.0 mm^2

16 AWG =   1.3 mm^2

etc ...

Tin-plated cable. Tin-plating is the process of adding a fine coating of tin (silver in aircraft), which protects the exposed copper against the oxidation that occurs in damp environments.

Halogen-free cable. This is a requirement from the classification agencies (e.g. Lloyd's, Norske Veritas) for commercial vessels. PVC (containing halogen chloride) generates corrosive gas onboard in a fire, which together with water creates a mist of hydrochloric acid. For a leisure boat a halogen-free cable is less important and far more expensive.

Cable terminals. Red, blue or yellow colour marks indicate the cable size that the cable clip is designed for. Red is for up to 1.5 mm^2, blue for 1.5–2.5 mm^2 and yellow for 2.6 6.0 mm^2.

Multi-wire cable. The more wires, the more flexible the cable. The thicker the cable, the more important the flexibility for easy installation in the boat.

Heat resistance. Cables have a heat-resistance rating, usually 70°C for single cables and 90°C for high-quality cables. This represents the temperature that the copper wire inside the cable can withstand, not the ambient temperature in the engine compartment, for example.

The cable expert Per Hjelm

Per Hjelm's company has been selling cables for more than 30 years, and he has met many boat owners during that time.

– For an ordinary leisure boat it is enough to use what we call a car/boat cable. This is a cheap, single, PVC-coated cable, and it is what the boatyards normally use for installations to keep the cost down, since few manufacturers want to make a more expensive boat than their competitors, says Per Hjelm, adding that customers do not usually request high-quality cables in their new boat.

If you need a higher specification, or you are going to sail across the oceans, Per recommends the same type of cable used by commercial vessels, because out there 'the sea demands it'.

Per is still a little puzzled as to why there are no legal specifications for cable types in leisure boats – not even from insurance companies. In the US, the ABYC (American Boat and Yacht Council) has established recommendations that we should be able to apply to European leisure boats. This cable is tin-plated, with a hard-grade PVC-blend coating (a measure of durability), and should withstand 600 V and have a heat resistance of 90°C.

A prerequisite for success is that all crimpings are gas-proof and for this it is recommended that you avoid the cheap cable crimper kit from the petrol station in favour of a good-quality hexagonal crimping tool.

PER'S TOP 5 TIPS

1. Use a good-quality cable (tin-plated copper cable, 90°C PVC and 600 V)

2. Crimp the cables properly.

3. Use Vaseline to protect against moisture.

4. Label and document the cabling carefully.

5. Make sure you protect main cables from chafe – at worst it could cause a fire or battery explosion.

HOW TO CRIMP YOUR CABLES

All terminals will need crimping. Please get a proper tool for this, since you will do a lot of crimping and every below standard crimp with a cheap tool may eventually cause problems. The better choice of a double-crimp ratchet tool can now be found for below £30 and will help even a novice to a perfect crimping.

The crimper will have marked crimping positions for the most commonly used terminals: red, blue and yellow for 1.5mm^2, 2.5mm^2 and 6mm^2 terminals.

To make a proper crimp between large diameter cable and tubular crimp a lug terminal is vital. You will need to get the correct size lug for the wire that you are using and will need a suitable crimping tool. Best is to use a manual hexagonal crimping tool that normally handles lug sizes between 6 and 50 mm with revolving dies. There

are dies up to 185 mm that can be made by hand, and then there are also hydraulic tools that can be rented or take larger diameter to a shop with the heavy machinery.

There are cheap hammer crimp tools that are not as exact or easy to use, as the hexagonal crimping tool.

It is also possible to solder lugs and terminals if you have the knowledge how to do that, but for a beginner a crimping tool is the best method by far.

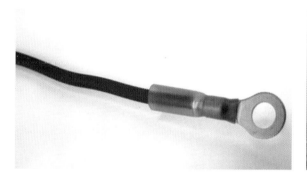

Strip the cable and place a terminal of the correct size on its end. Shrink terminals have melting glue that will form a watertight connection.

The ratchet crimping tool gives a perfect crimp on the terminal.

The plastic of the shrink terminal is heated (with a small gas burner) to shrink onto the cable and terminal.

For extra security (or if normal terminals are being used) a shrink tube can be added, along with a plastic label to identify the cable.

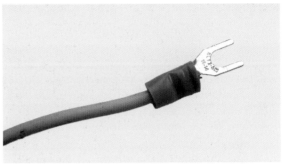

A cheap crimper, like the one used on this cable end, will not yield good results in the long run.

A ratchet crimping tool with a release block will ensure properly crimped cable clips every time.

Below: A double-crimp ratchet tool uses gearing to compress the terminal, and the ratchet does not release until the cable clip is correctly crimped.

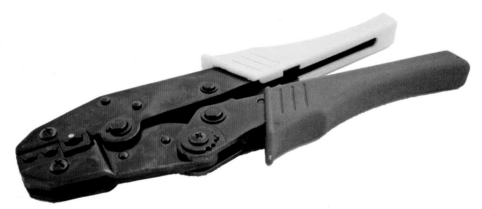

Lugs for battery cables of different quality. The example in the middle is to be avoided. These lugs are for crimping, even if it's possible to solder them too.

It is very important that the battery terminal lugs are perfectly crimped. I could pull Roobarb's old lugs right off.

Project: Crimp your cables

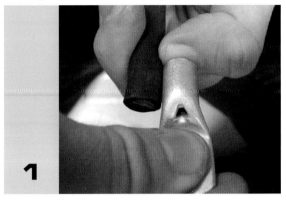

1

▲ Measure with the lug how much of the insulation needs to be stripped from the wire so that the wire fits into the lug.

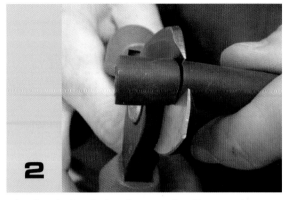

2

▲ Cut the insulation. Do not strip off too much insulation or you will see a gap between the lug and the insulation material.

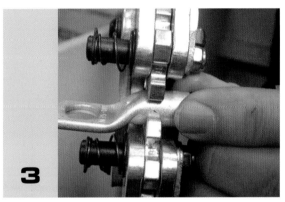

3

▲ Place the lug in to the correct crimping location in the tool, push the cable as far as possible into the lug and then squeeze the handles together as hard as possible. Make two crimps on each lug.

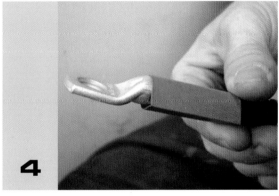

4

▲ Put a piece of heat shrinking tube onto the cable. Heat shrinking will reduce the tube's diameter by 300% or sometimes more.

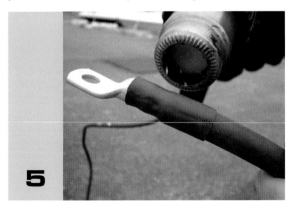

5

▲ Use a heat gun or torch to shrink it into place, this will make the cable-lug crimp almost waterproof. For extra protection use glue-lined shrink tube.

6

▲ Put some waterfree Vaseline on all exposed metal parts of your connections to protect them from corrosion.

04

BATTERIES

BATTERIES

Essentially, if you are a pedantic boat owner and look after your batteries well, normal open type marine/leisure batteries are the most cost effective – as long as you take into account that they need to be replaced every few years. But since these batteries are relatively cheap, they do give better capacity per pound/dollar.

However, if you are going blue water cruising, or need a great deal of reliable power on board, and you are dependent upon the batteries keeping their charge for long periods, then – as long as you care for them exactly according to the instructions – the more expensive types are preferable (lithium-ion, gel, spiral-wound, AGM- or 'truck' batteries).

The newer types of batteries have a better specification, hold more charge for less weight, are more tolerant to deep levels of discharge, and charge and discharge faster and for more cycles.

The battery guide at the end of this chapter tells you what all this means.

MY CHOICE

As I planned to cruise the oceans with the rather small *Roobarb*, I chose two AGM-type batteries of 100 Ah each, which are connected in parallel and – in theory – hold 200 Ah together. For a long-distance sailing boat, that is not a lot; but I planned to generate extra power from a small wind generator and two solar cells that should contribute 30–50% of the daily power consumption (if it is windy or sunny). Another consideration was that there was only space available for two batteries in the 'house bank'.

A choice of batteries must be made, but do not listen too much to the salesmen telling you to get the top-of-the-line products. Often the cheap modern open cell lead batteries are enough for coastal cruising during the summer ...

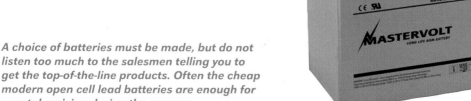

CHOOSING CAPACITY

A battery's capacity is measured in ampere hours (Ah). The greater the Ah, the more power the battery will hold, enabling it to supply energy for a longer period. However, a wet cell battery should preferably not be drained of more than 50 per cent (30 % is even better) of its charge. I estimated daily consumption at around 45 Ah – that is, approximately 25 per cent of the total capacity – which is a fairly appropriately calculated battery bank. The biggest consumers are the refrigerator, computer/plotter and the lighting/nav lights on board *Roobarb* when sailing.

CONNECTING

During the project, I noticed that many installation instructions, such as for bilge pumps, refrigerator etc, recommend that the cables to the power supply are connected directly to the battery.

I can imagine that this is to prevent potential problems (and warranty issues), due to the fact that corroded cables with too little capacity and other system losses mean that the products do not work as well as stated in the brochures. And this is possibly why the manufacturers recommend that you skip as many uncertain factors as possible. Maybe so...

Anatomy of a battery. A cross-section through an AGM battery showing the different plates separated by glassfibre mats and grids pasted with an active material that produces power in combination with an electrolyte through a chemical process.

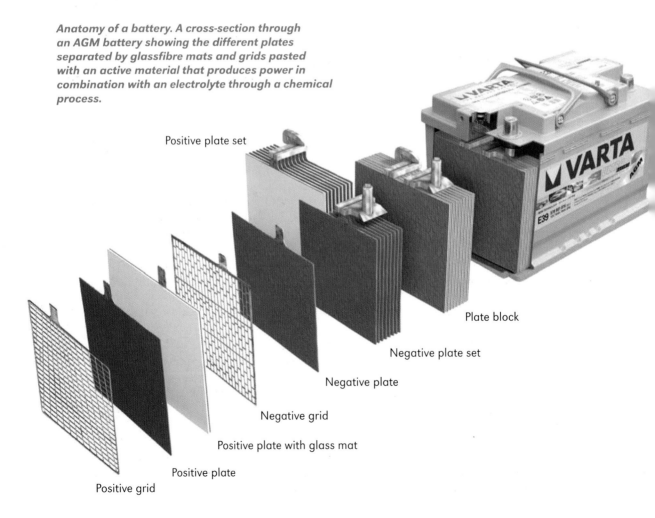

Positive plate set

Plate block

Negative plate set

Negative plate

Negative grid

Positive plate with glass mat

Positive plate

Positive grid

Roobarb's electrical system is constructed not to present any major loss of voltage. This is why I am changing all cables, and upgrading wherever possible. I want to connect most of the consumers to the terminal blocks on the distribution box, rather than the battery poles.

In spite of this, there are several cables attached to each battery pole – charger, battery meter, etc. The more equipment, the bigger the problem these direct connections to the battery must be, since not only one but several manufacturers recommend this.

UPSIDE DOWN

Batteries (and chargers) should, according to the safety recommendations (CE regulations on new boats), preferably be housed in their own compartment, separated from engine and fuel tanks. If you have open cells, oxyhydrogen gas is produced and in that case the compartment needs to be ventilated. Open batteries should also be placed in acid-resistant boxes (epoxy-coated plywood boxes are fine).

It is also important that the batteries are properly secured. Stainless-steel mounts and strong straps are the simplest way. On *Roobarb* I have made sure that the batteries stay in place, even if the boat turns upside down.

The large battery bank weighs almost 75 kilos, and apart from the box that prevents the batteries from sliding sideways if the boat heels heavily, I have also laminated bolts straight onto the hull with a strong strap (which I have pulled to test) to hold the batteries in place, almost whatever happens.

I screwed the storage battery to the bottom plate with stainless-steel screws and large washers. This means that when the batteries need replacing, I must either get the same size batteries or make new fittings.

METERING BATTERY STATUS

There are many different digital 'tank meters' on the market, from simple voltmeters to sophisticated processor-driven miracles that can keep track of almost anything.

A battery meter makes it easier for the boat owner to keep track of the battery status, if you are dependent on your batteries.

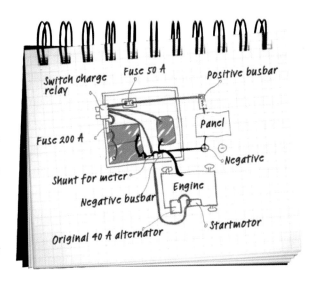

Making a first drawing of how the cables would be laid, with all the measurements and a list of how much to buy of everything, made it a lot easier. In the end there were a lot of drawings of the various system parts.

For *Roobarb*, who will spend a lot of time at sea, a battery meter will be very useful, although the cost is a couple of hundred pounds on top of everything else that needed to be replaced in the electrical system.

If you only sail along the coast and also have access to shore power in marinas and at your own berth, it is doubtful whether there is any point in having one on board.

Read more about meters in the fact box.

BATTERY CABLES

It is important to have sufficient cable diameter – the thicker the cable, the better. Possibly the only thing that would prevent us using thick cables throughout, is the high price per metre for heavier-duty cables (and perhaps that it may be difficult to fit them in, as they will be pulled through bulkheads and other obstructions).

If the battery banks are fairly close to the engine and the alternator, use 35 mm^2, otherwise you have to use a larger dimension. Refer to the ready reckoner in the previous chapter, or ask the chandler for the right cable size.

Also use heavy-duty cable (both on the positive and negative side) to the terminal blocks on the distribution box. I used 35 mm^2 for that too, as I had a whole roll of cable available. A diameter of 16 mm^2 would also have been fine for the just over 1 metre distance between the battery and the block.

FUSES

It is quite uncommon to use fuses with heavy-duty cables, but it is thoroughly recommended. The main fuses should be positioned close to the battery for maximum protection. You need large fuses: 100–400 A (up to 750 A are available) in special fuse holders. Use a 100 A fuse for the consumer bank and 400 A for the start battery, normally placed on the positive cable, but ideally on both...

At the distribution box, the plain fuses will protect the various consumers.

Circuit breakers for domestic use also work well for 12 V, and that is what I chose for *Roobarb*. Even blade fuses are fine, since they are designed for the often harsh automotive environment.

Older type automotive porcelain fuses, often found in boats from the 1970s, are not as good because they corrode easily. Electronics often have integrated fuses, mostly of glass.

If you have 'disposable' fuses that burn out, you must have plenty of spares on board. I spent a hot and humid half day in Holland a few years ago, searching desperately for fuses before I found the right size in a small shop several kilometres away...

SEPARATING THE BATTERIES

You need to be able to isolate the two (sometimes more) battery banks so that they do not discharge each other when you are not using the boat. The simplest way is to control them manually with a switch when charging.

Unfortunately, it is easy to forget to set them in the right position after charging and then you are back to the same problem of one bank depleting the other; but there are various aids on the market to help with monitoring this.

Twenty years ago, split charge diodes were the most common thing used, but the drawback with those is that they create a voltage drop of around 0.7 V and thus less charge.

Nowadays, a microprocessor separating relay is the usual method, and this works by interconnecting the batteries when they reach a certain voltage. Then, as the voltage in the batteries drops, the relay switches off and the batteries have no contact with each other. Sounds simple, but the problem

The voltage-sensitive relay built into this battery switch allows two batteries to be charged at the same time. When the engine is started and the start battery reaches 13.7 volts, the relay engages, allowing two battery banks (start and house) to be charged simultaneously.

This is a separate relay that will keep your batteries charged. Although there is debate over what is the best method, a relay is at least one of the most convenient.

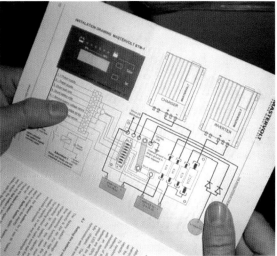

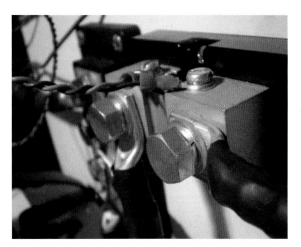

A battery meter can be a good tool for monitoring how much charge is left in the batteries.

Right, top: The manual for the battery meter, which we had to study closely before we understood exactly how to connect the five cables to the batteries and the shunt.

Right: The shunt is a measurement tool that is used to calculate the amperage consumed by a boat's various devices. As the current runs through the shunt, a small voltage is generated which is proportional to the current flow, which a battery monitor then calculates as a meter reading. The shunt is best placed close to the battery bank, and on the negative cable. A twisted cable is run to the monitor. The shunt consumes only a fraction of an ampere.

You can also use two screws in the battery cable set at a precise distance, to keep the cost down.

is to choose from the sales pitch of numerous manufacturers, and that is not easy.

There is also purely electronic charge distribution, which has no relay contacts or other automation and has very little internal resistance, with the drawback of being quite pricey.

KEEPING TRACK OF BATTERY BANK STATUS

In your new system it can be helpful to install a meter that will tell you the status of the battery banks. They range from a very simple voltmeter to sophisticated microprocessor-driven units that can keep track of almost anything.

The simplest solution is the hand-held voltmeter or multimeter directly on the battery, but you need to know how to interpret its readings. A voltmeter can only show roughly the battery status when the battery banks are not under load (i.e. not used for the last 24 hours).

A full lead cell battery, when not in use, normally has a voltage of approximately 12.7–12.8 V, and an empty battery is approximately one volt lower (see box page 57).

A simple voltmeter can provide some important information about the charging voltage, which is vital for charging a battery fully. How high the level of charging voltage should be depends on the battery type, usually around 14.4–14.7 V.

In a small boat the electrical system can be kept to a minimum. This is a First 21.7 I sailed for seven weeks from the west coast of France to the Baltic and Sweden. It lacked some creature comforts, but we did all right and didn't miss them too much.

Metering

A more advanced and also more expensive battery meter is an instrument that, apart from voltage and power, also shows how many ampere hours (Ah) have been used since the battery was full, or how many Ah are currently left.

Some battery meters also show the percentage of capacity currently in the battery. The percentage is much easier to understand, since you don't need to know how large the battery bank is. But this normally means programming and reading the manual...

For a consumption of 5 A during 10 hours, 50 Ah have been used, and if the battery is 200 Ah (e.g. like *Roobarb*'s battery bank), there is 75 per cent left. During consumption, this is easy to show as, in simple terms, the instrument constantly measures the power and multiplies it by the time.

When charging, however, it is much more complicated, because the battery's conversion efficiency is not 100 per cent. Therefore, when charging, the instrument measures the power and multiplies it by the time, and divides/multiplies it by the conversion efficiency factor.

Conversion efficiency

The conversion efficiency is vital to how precisely the instrument will show what is currently left in the battery, or how much has been used for every moment since the battery was full.

Some instruments have a preset conversion efficiency, for example 90 per cent. Such an instrument must be reset manually now and then, in order to show the correct reading.

A digital battery meter can be a useful tool to monitor how much charge is left in the batteries. Not to be confused with a voltmeter.

Other instruments have an easily adjustable conversion efficiency, which thus can be adapted according to battery type, age, charge, use, etc, for better precision.

The best instruments calculate the conversion efficiency themselves by, among other things, taking into account when the charging current drops below a certain level at the same time as the voltage rises above a certain level. And when this happens, the instrument automatically resets, provided that all ampere hours are recharged.

Then the processor can calculate the new conversion efficiency to be used until the battery is fully charged. Limit values for voltage and current must be adjustable, so that the instrument can be adapted to all battery types and the boat's charging system.

History

A good battery meter should also be able to show some historical data, such as: deepest discharge in Ah, mean discharge, number of charging cycles, total discharges, times the instrument has been synchronized, times of low and high voltage alarm. These resets data can be used, among other things, for diagnostics, and if you want to evaluate your batteries to see when they need replacing.

FOCUS   TYPES OF BATTERY

OPEN CELL BATTERIES

A leisure/marine battery is a flooded (unsealed) 12 V lead-acid battery, with slightly thicker lead plates than ordinary car starter batteries, and can therefore withstand deeper discharges.

The relatively low price is the greatest advantage of marine and leisure batteries, and they give you the most power for money, so despite a shorter life expectancy than more expensive batteries, it may be the best choice for any boat used only for a few weeks every summer.

(+) Relatively cheap

(+) Can withstand deep discharge

(-) Maintenance – must be refilled with distilled water now and then

(-) Can produce hazardous oxyhydrogen gas if overcharged

(-) Can spill acid if tipped over

GEL BATTERIES

The 'gel' refers to the addition of silica gel to the sulphuric acid in the battery. This type is suitable as a domestic battery because it can withstand many charge cycles, even more than AGM batteries. Leak-proof.

(+) Can withstand many charge cycles

(+) Low self-discharge

(+) Maintenance free

(-) Heavy

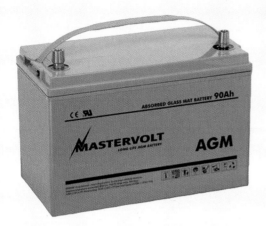

ABSORBED GLASS MAT

In AGM batteries, the acid is absorbed in glass-fibre mats between the plates to avoid leakage. AGM batteries can accept higher charging voltages and many charging cycles.

Well suited for storage batteries, inverters, anchor winches or bow propellers, which require high currents.

Can be fitted upside down or sideways, if you like.

(+) Can withstand many charge cycles (but fewer than gel)

(+) Low self-discharge

(+) Maintenance free

(-) Heavy

SEMI TRACTION BATTERIES

Also known as 'golf cart' batteries and used in, among other things, electric trucks and golf carts, which are deeply discharged every day for years.

Often in the shape of 2 V cells, which are connected in series of six to form a 12 V cell. Can have high capacities – 1200 Ah is not unusual. They are large and heavy and suit bigger boats; they are popular with long-distance sailors, since they tolerate deep discharges very well.

(+) Can withstand an extreme number of charge cycles

(+) Up to 10–15 years of life

(+) Low self-discharge

(-) Very expensive and heavy

SPIRAL-WOUND BATTERIES

This type has the lead in the plates fixed in a spiral, which results in a larger flat surface and the plates closer together, with a low internal resistance. It's based on AGM batteries and is well suited as engine/starter batteries, because it generates a lot of power. Tolerates shaking and vibration to a greater extent.

(+) Generates a lot of power

(+) Tolerates vibrations

(+) Can withstand high charge

(-) Expensive

TYPES OF BATTERY continued

LITHIUM-ION BATTERIES

Lithium-ion batteries are a new technology we are already seeing more of. Until recently you were most likely to find them in mobile phones and digital cameras. The pros are that they are much lighter, about one-third the weight of a lead cell battery, and can take many and deep discharges. They can also easily be charged up to 90–94 per cent of their capacity (for a lead cell it can be as low as 70–85 per cent), but require good charging supervision. Lasts three times as long as open, but also costs about three times more than normal marine lead-cell type batteries. Prices will drop as more producers pick up the technology. The first versions of the Li-ion demanded very specific charging and needed special chargers to manage each cell individually.

(+) Can charge up to 2,000 cycles

(+) Very little self discharge (typically 10 per cent for 12 months)

(+) Light (compared to older type batteries)

(-) Need advanced individual charging per each cell

(-) Still expensive

FUEL CELL

A process converts the chemical energy from a fuel (normally methanol in yachts) into electricity through a chemical reaction with oxygen, the emissions are carbon dioxide and water. The efficiency of a fuel cell is in general between 40-60 %. The weight of the unit is normally below 10 kg.

Fuel cells are becoming more popular and can help keep the load on the batteries small or charge them overnight. Around 100-200 Ah or more per 24 hours is now common.

Fuel cells are fast coming down in price as more units are produced for a broader market.

(+) Gives a low but constant charge

(+) Low emissions

(-) Still expensive

Test your batteries

Most batteries fail slowly from natural aging processes and use. Occasionally, but rarely, batteries fail suddenly as a result of mechanical damage or a defect.

The main aging processes are sulphation, when crystals of sulphate builds up over a period of time when the battery is left in a discharged condition or because of infrequent use. Some modern chargers can shock the battery (sometimes called 'reconditioning') with a very high voltage to boil the electrolyte in the battery. This takes its toll but may give another few months of use in a battery that would otherwise need replacing.

The other process is dehydration of the battery by overcharging. This is when the water in the electrolyte is gassing and the fluid level goes down and corrosion of the plates starts. In an open battery you can refill destilled water, but in a 'maintenance-free' battery you cannot. So in that sense a closed cell battery needs more care. Especially since they most often are more expensive.

To test a battery's health it is not enough to use a multimeter - you will need a battery tester that will put a load on the battery to check the internal workings.

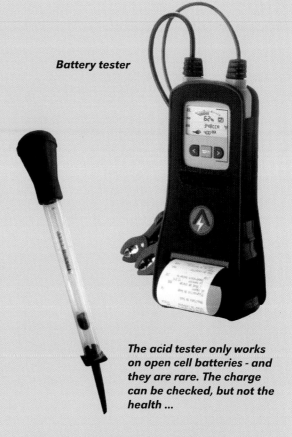

Battery tester

The acid tester only works on open cell batteries - and they are rare. The charge can be checked, but not the health ...

The exact technique differs between manufacturers, but get a quality one.

But, borrow or rent a battery tester if you are suspicious of the remaining life of your batteries.

Measuring battery charge

In its simplest form, you have a voltmeter (digital or analogue multimeter) that measures the voltage in the battery. The disadvantage is that the battery can't be under load (and should preferably have been at rest for the last 24 hours) to get the correct reading. So this is not a good method during the holidays.

12.75 V 100 %

12.48 V 70 %

12.24 V 40 %

12.00 V 10 %

11.63 V Empty

(Open cell lead type battery, at 20°C and not in use)

Project:
Replace your battery

PROJECT FACTS

DIFFICULTY: easy

TIME: approx. 15 hours

COST: 3 batteries about £700, cable 10 meters x 35 mm² £80, lugs, shrink tubing etc £20, battery separator BEP 716-SQ inclusive relay £140, battery meter from Mastervolt £550.

TOOLS: Crimper for lugs can be hired from some chandlers.

1

▲ My first idea was to position the batteries low, near the engine room in the bilge (the shallow part), and in waterproof boxes. However, there was not enough space for two 100 Ah batteries.

2

▲ Instead I epoxied a platform to the inside of one of the dinette settees, adjacent to the engine. I took out the settee first, to make more room to work.

3

▲ I also laminated two new bulkheads in the box, to provide some surfaces for mounting chargers and other things.

4

▲ I searched the market for batteries that would also suit long-distance sailing. For the storage battery I chose a spiral-wound 55 Ah and for the consumer bank, two 100 Ah AGM.

5

▲ I tested several different solutions for how best to fit the batteries in the new box before I was satisfied with the placement.

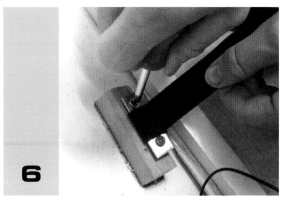

6

▲ I screwed strong straps securely to wooden blocks, strongly epoxied to the hull. I tested all the straps by pulling them hard.

7

▲ Next it was time to start making the right number of cables of appropriate size. Cutting, crimping, coating with a little Vaseline and pulling on shrink tubing.

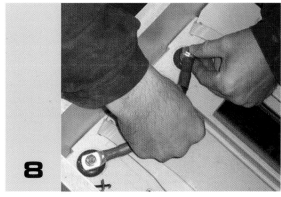

8

▲ All cables fitted in the battery box were of 35mm^2.

9

▲ The outside surfaces of cable clips and battery terminals were also treated to a thin Vaseline coating, to prevent corrosion in the long term.

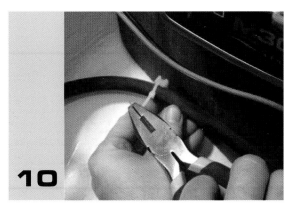

10

▲ All cables are fixed to the bulkheads, using various methods – with bundle straps or inserted in plastic tubes.

11

▲ The switches I set into the side of the box, to enable me to switch on the power easily when I get into the boat.

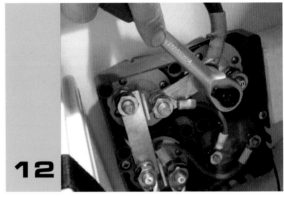

12

▲ The switches and relay are in a cluster. The relay connects the battery banks at 13.7 V charge voltage, and disconnects at 12.8 V.

13

▲ I originally made my own terminal blocks from a piece of plastic and a stainless bolt, which only cost a few pence. In the end I bought new ones.

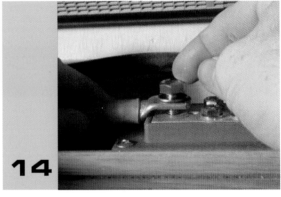

14

▲ The positive cable (35 mm^2) from the consumer bank is connected to the block in the electricity cabinet behind the distribution box. A 16 mm^2 cable runs from here to the fuses.

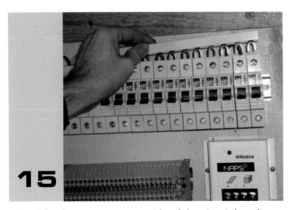

15

▲ A busbar connects one side of the circuit breakers, which are then allocated to the switches for the various consumers in the boat.

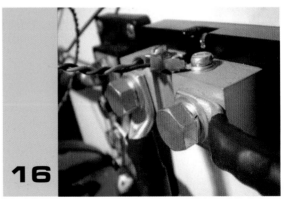

16

▲ The shunt should be installed according to the manual, with the charger connected to the busbar after the shunt to be able to calculate the charge.

▲ Inside the meter I needed to connect the different ports, which I only realized after a careful reading of the rather complicated manual.

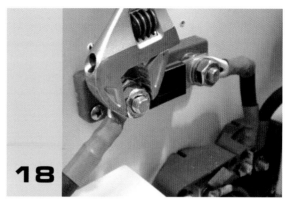

▲ The fuses in the positive cables were placed as close to the batteries as possible.

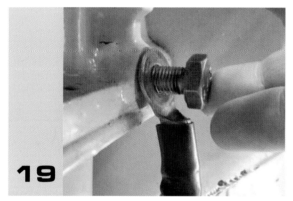

▲ Finally, we also connected the batteries' negative side to the engine block casting, with a (hard to find) fine-pitch bolt.

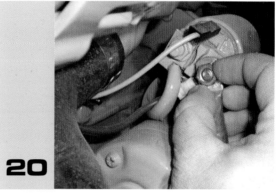

▲ The starter motor relay is connected to the storage battery's positive side and is also joined to the generator, which has a shorter piece of cable for the starter motor (the thin red cable was later replaced by a 35 mm² cable).

▲ The battery meter shows the charging voltage and the up-to-date status of the batteries. The meter needs some programming before all its features can be used.

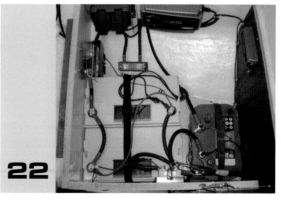

▲ Most components are in position in the battery box. Two battery banks house the 200 Ah and the 55 Ah spiral-wound start battery for cranking the engine.

Terminology on board

A battery contains a series of connected cells, which produce power through a chemical process. One cell consists of a positive electrode, an intermediate electrolyte (often absorbed in a porous separator) and a negative electrode.

Really called an **accumulator**, as it can be recharged.

Deep discharge is when the battery has been emptied by 50–80 per cent of its total capacity. A lead-acid battery will survive considerably longer if not discharged to more than about 30 per cent of its capacity.

The consumer battery is the bank that usually has the largest number of batteries and supplies all the boat's daily consumers, such as the refrigerator, lighting, nav lights, etc.

Charge cycles, i.e. the number of times a battery can withstand being recharged, ranging from 50 for a storage battery to several hundred for the more expensive batteries. The more a battery is discharged before recharging, the fewer cycles it can take – could be 200 cycles at 100 per cent discharge, for example, but 900 cycles at 30 per cent discharge.

The Peukert coefficient ('k') describes the decreased capacity available in a lead–acid battery the higher the rate at which it is discharged. The battery will become flatter the more amperes you take out – thus a 5 A rate for 10 hours is better for the battery than a 50 A load for one hour. The Peukert coefficient varies according to the age of the battery, generally increasing with age.

Parallel connection is when more than one battery is joined together to achieve a higher capacity with a sustainable current in a consumer bank. Use batteries of the same make, model and age, because discrepancies can discharge the batteries.

A storage battery should withstand a high load within a very short time. It is never discharged, but is charged directly by the engine.

Valve regulation (valve regulated lead acid battery, VRLA) means that it is a sealed system. Therefore the batteries can be placed upside down, if you wish. They do not need and cannot be filled with distilled water, but in case of heavy overcharge, there is often a relief valve that lets out gas.

Self-discharge is when the battery loses its current in storage or without recharging, by 1–15 per cent per month. Some batteries (e.g. AGM) can be stored for up to a year without recharging.

'Sulphating' is when lead sulphate is formed on both the positive and negative electrode through absorption of the sulphuric acid in the electrolyte. Some modern battery chargers have a reconditioning mode, where higher charging voltages make the batteries 'gas', and thus release the sulphate.

Winter storage A fully charged lead-acid battery can tolerate -65°C and therefore be left in the boat over winter, possibly charging once or twice during that time. A completely empty battery can tolerate -10°C before it is destroyed by the cold.

Open batteries are the most common type of boat batteries, especially storage batteries. They should be maintained (filled with battery water), cannot withstand being tilted too much, and can produce dangerous oxyhydrogen gas if overcharged.

Batteries are often consumables. Look after them and they will last longer. When their life has ended, make sure they are dealt with appropriately at a recycling centre.

05
CHARGING

>> CHARGING

I have heard several analogies made to explain battery charging. One is that it is like feeding an infant – the fuller the baby gets, the harder it is to get any food into it. Another compares it to filling a glass to the brim with water – the nearer the top, the slower you must pour not to spill any.

The reality is that charging batteries until completely full is a rather slow process, because charging the last few percent requires a long time. It is quite quick to charge a battery to 80–85 per cent of its capacity, but the remaining 15–20 percent takes a long time (8–16 hours), regardless of what type of charger is used. The battery resists, which means that most batteries rarely get fully charged. Normally they are only 85 per cent full.

THE ALTERNATOR

A larger alternator can charge faster than a smaller one, but at a cost – it needs a high rpm before it starts to charge, and then steals power from the propulsion. The rather feeble 40 A alternator that was supplied as standard with my new Vetus engine loses me about 1 horsepower (hp) of the engine power, while a 115 A, as supplied with Volvo's new small engines, steals about 2 hp.

The disadvantage of a large alternator is that it needs a high rpm before it starts to charge.

The disadvantages of a small alternator are that it takes longer to charge the batteries and there is a great risk that they will never be fully charged out at sea (one possible solution is to visit a marina every now and then to charge at 230 V).

The alternator contains a control function – the regulator – that provides the batteries with the correct voltage. This can sometimes be improved with an external regulator, but at a cost.

However, modern batteries have somewhat different requirements, and it is not definite that the integrated control can handle even new batteries – particularly in hot (or cold) climates. But for that there are external control devices available to regulate the charge.

Good-quality aftermarket alternators are expensive, more than £1,000–1,300 if you want a sophisticated model, which is perhaps more than most leisure boat owners are prepared to pay.

The brackets needed for a new alternator may need heavy modification. Before buying, check that you can actually fit the unit on to your engine and/or your engine compartment.

Some boat owners have installed a car alternator, which is less expensive but then needs some modification in the installation. They are therefore not the best choice for a first-time installation, unless you get help from someone with the right experience.

DIFFERENT CHARGE REQUIREMENTS

The battery banks – starting and domestic – should ideally be charged separately, as they have different characteristics and often different types of batteries. A starting battery is in use for a short period and does not have time to discharge to any great extent. The domestic bank, which may be large (in terms of the number of Ah), is regularly deeply discharged, and may need a long time to recharge. It is not possible to charge separately with a single alternator so you must provide some way to separate the battery banks. Split charge diodes used to be the norm 20 years ago, but modern technology has better solutions where the loss of power is less.

With a shore power charger, you can use two different battery chargers to provide different types of charge, a solution I used on *Roobarb*.

BATTERY CHARGERS

These days battery chargers are very sophisticated devices. If you have an old car battery charger, with a tiny trembling needle on a voltmeter, a replacement is long overdue. A modern charger charges in several phases. Three-phase chargers are common, but now there are also eight-phase chargers.

I do not in any way presume to understand how you determine which charger is the best, but from the advice I received I can summarize the following guidelines as a starting point for choosing a charger:

1. You get what you pay for. A good charger is not cheap – be prepared to pay £250–300 or more.
2. The capacity should be approximately 10–30 per cent of the battery capacity, e.g. 20–60 A for a 200 Ah battery bank.
3. The best chargers are able to sense the battery temperature and adapt the charge accordingly.

Based on these guidelines, I chose two separate chargers for the battery banks on *Roobarb*. One is a bigger, 25 A charger that charges the domestic bank rather efficiently. It has a temperature sensor, which is attached to the consumer bank's negative side and regulates the charge according to the battery temperature without overheating. The charger also contains a cooling fan, which means that it must be positioned away from any splashing water, but there are waterproof chargers available if required.

In addition to this, the boat has a little 0.8 A charger, which charges the small amount needed for the starter battery.

The argument for having two different chargers seems logical, as it appears to be a real problem to manage two banks of totally different size and charge characteristics with one charger. But opinions differ among battery charger manufacturers and you will probably find contradictory advice.

MULTI-STAGE CHARGING

With most modern 230 V battery chargers, there are three charging phases: bulk, absorption and float charging. There are chargers that divide these phases into several smaller parts, and also include other features, such as reconditioning the battery.

Bulk charging is the first phase. Current is applied to the battery to the maximum safe rate until the voltage reaches around 80–90 per cent of full charge level. The voltage normally varies between 10.5 and 15 V, depending on the type of battery.

The second stage charges at a constant voltage, gradually reducing the current as the battery's internal resistance increases during charging. Now the charger supplies the highest voltage, normally around 14.2 to 15.5 V.

Float or trickle charging is the third phase. When the battery is fully charged, the charging voltage is reduced to around 12.8–13.4 V, which reduces gassing and prolongs the battery's life by keeping it topped up. The method used can be impulse charging, where short charge pulses provide charging.

These chargers have microprocessors to regulate this and prevent both over- and undercharging.

Some chargers offer a reconditioning function, where an extra high charge current is applied to the battery to make it 'gas' – producing bubbles in the electrolyte/hydrochloric acid. This helps to remix it and can make a bad battery better. However, it is a method to be used with caution, since it also causes wear on the batteries, and sealed batteries cannot be refilled with battery water, which will evaporate when the acid produces gas.

FOCUS CHARGE CYCLES

There is a limit how many times you can recharge your batteries - the deeper the discharge the less life you can expect from your battery. Ideally, as discussed earlier in the book, the charge of a battery should never go below 70 percent.

A good quality battery will withstand hundreds of charge cycles, but will eventually lose capacity and will need to be replaced. And quality batteries are expensive and should all be replaced at the same time.

Right: The life expectancy of a maintenance-free deep-cycle AGM battery from Uplus. DOD is 'depth of discharge'.

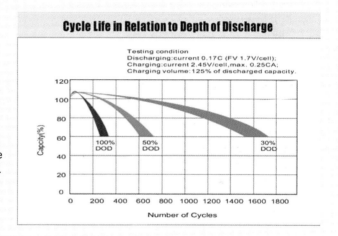

Cycle Life in Relation to Depth of Discharge

Testing condition
Discharging:current 0.17C (FV 1.7V/cell);
Charging:current 2.45V/cell,max. 0.25CA;
Charging volume:125% of discharged capacity.

FOCUS CHARGE CONTROLLERS

A charge controller can be a good investment since it will make the charging of your battery banks from the engine's alternator more effective, thus saving on fuel and cost by not having to run the engine for hours to top up the batteries.

A charge controller limits the rate at which electric current is put into the battery. Pulse width modulation (PWM) and maximum power point tracker (MPPT) technologies are more electronically sophisticated, adjusting charging rates depending on the battery's level, to allow charging closer to its maximum capacity. Charge controllers may also monitor battery temperature to prevent overheating. Some charge controller systems also display data, transmit data to remote displays, and data logging to track electricity flow over time.

A charge controller is also necessary to regulate the DC current from solar panels, as this is can be too high to charge a 12 volt battery.

Guide: Trickle charge and other charging methods

A modern AC charger will most likely have functions to keep the battery banks happy. First it will keep an eye on the main or bulk charge to make this efficient without harming the battery. Too much or too little can cause problems and, if too much, it may gas the battery and if it's sealed there is no way to top up the electrolyte and you may end up having to buy a new expensive battery.

Take care of your expensive batteries - it's a very effective way to save money. Instead of waxing and buffing the hull, spend that on a quality charger and make sure to charge at regular intervals even when the boat is not in use (in the winter for instance).

FOCUS

WHEN IS A BATTERY DISCHARGED?

A battery bank's available capacity is about half of what is stated on the batteries (rated capacity). If there are three 70 Ah leisure batteries in the consumer bank, you can use three times 70 Ah (210 Ah) divided by two, i.e. 105 Ah.

If the charge level falls below that, it is what is commonly called a 'deep discharge'. A battery can only stand that a certain number of times. Different battery types tolerate a different number of deeper discharges before losing capacity, when they will need replacing. Discharging the battery too deeply is the quickest and most common way of killing your expensive batteries.

It is better to recharge early, rather than wait until the domestic bank is depleted. Wind- or solar-energy charging makes good sense to keep your batteries happy and long-lived.

When recharging from your sailboat's engine and its alternator, the battery bank is seldom charged to more than 80-85% of its capacity (15-20% discharged), and the available capacity is actually only about 30-35% of the battery's capacity.

In the calculation above, this means that, with a 210 Ah bank, around 65 Ah is available. This would be enough for *Roobarb*'s daily power needs, according to my first electricity budget (see chapter 2).

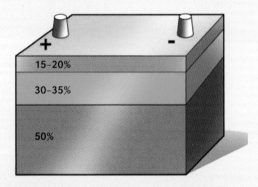

15-20% This is what the alternator on the engine does NOT manage to charge on a normal charge run. In a 110 Ah battery it is about 15-17 Ah.

30-35% This is the available capacity in a wet cell battery – only about a third of the capacity should be used, as a deep discharge may harm the battery. On a 110 Ah battery, this gives about a 40 Ah range from charged to discharged.

50% This is the minimum capacity that should be left in the battery in order to prolong its life. On a 110 Ah battery it is about 55 Ah.

Read more on testing your batteries on page 57.

Project: Install a battery charger

▲ The kit came with two chargers: the big 25 A charger takes care of the house bank and the smaller, separate 0.8 A charger keeps the start battery topped up

▲ I had to widen the fixed cable clips on the charger to fit the screw terminal blocks on the batteries.

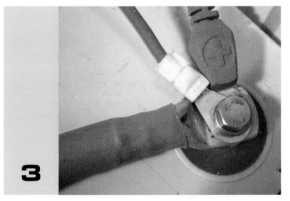

▲ The battery charger's positive lead is connected directly to the screw terminal blocks on the battery bank. The terminal is a 6 mm screw that makes it easy to connect equipment when needed.

▲ The negative lead from the charger goes to the busbar next to the shunt to make it possible to meter the charge in the consumer bank. The charger's temperature sensor is placed on the battery.

▲ The house bank charger shows the charging progress and also has different programmes for, among other things, a fanless night mode and reconditioning.

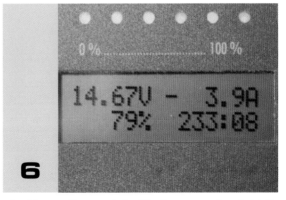

▲ The monitor needed a bit of programming, but tells me the status of the two groups. This is under charge.

06

SHORE POWER

SHORE POWER

It can be practical to include shore power in your boat's electrical system to enable you to charge and completely top up the batteries from the mains. Since 230 V can be lethal, however, I would strongly suggest considering a Plug and Play system, which greatly reduces the risk of making a potentially hazardous mistake when installing shore power.

As a (European) boat owner, according to EU Recreational Craft Directive (RCD) 94/25/EC and 2003/44/EC* and the international standard EN ISO 13297, you do not need to be a licensed electrician, but must have the 'required knowledge' to install a 230 V system (as opposed to a Plug and Play one). This applies only to private 'small craft' – if the boat is to be used in any way commercially, then there are strict regulations. In the US, you must adhere to the ABYC set of regulations.

This RCD is somewhat vague in the area of AC and is, unfortunately, rather open to interpretation. What is quite certain, however, is that if someone gets injured on a boat from the shore power system, the owner takes full responsibility. This is why I recommend that you consider a ready-made system, which does not involve any crimping or exposed wire ends – it's one of those situations when it's better to avoid DIY. To use a Plug and Play system will greatly reduce the stress of potentially doing something wrong, even though it is a bit more expensive. I looked upon this extra cost as life insurance...

There are a few different manufacturers of Plug and Play systems – they are all quite similar, but unfortunately most are not interchangeable as they use different plugs. DEFA, Mastervolt, CTEK, Ratio, TBB Power and a few others supply this type of system.

The systems normally include an IP-classed (Ingress Protection, waterproofness) inlet, with a twist-lock connector to make a safe and waterproof connection. The central cabinet should include a 30mA residual current device (a 10mA RCD is much more sensitive, but not common) and also possibly a galvanic isolator, popularly called a 'zinc saver'. Then it is safe to connect outlets and to connect to the battery charger(s).

---

* These EU Recreational Craft Directives (RCDs) are implemented in the UK as Recreational Craft Regulations 2004 (SI 2004/1464) and the Recreational Craft (Amendment) Regulations 2004 (SI 2004/3201). At the time of writing, these regulations were under revision, so I would strongly recommend that you research current guidelines before embarking on any such projects.

INSTALLING THE SYSTEM

Everything was delivered in a couple of boxes and since all that was required was pushing the connectors together, the installation was very easy – not originally intended for DIY, but rather for boat builders to save time and money on the installation.

I chose to place the inlet inside a storage box in the cockpit coaming since it was very close to where the stainless steel inlet could fit and also close to the battery compartment where the chargers would be.

EARTH THE SYSTEM

There are a couple of questions that may not have a straightforward answer.

The ground/earth from the shore-based system should also be installed on board, but can cause many problems. My recommendation is to connect the onboard AC systems to a common ground/earth, separate entirely from the shore-based one.

The best solution is to install a heavy iron-core isolation transformer that prevents the shore AC ground/earth from coming onboard.

220, 230 or 240 Volts?

The voltage from your domestic outlet is what we normally call 220 V (110 V in the US), although in reality it is around 230–240 V.

In marinas especially, it is not uncommon for the voltage to drop the further out on the pontoons you are – it can drop below 200 V and may cause problems with AC equipment, or even destroy it.

An alternative solution may be to use a 10mA ground circuit breaker, which will detect any leakage and break the power when it detects a difference in the voltage. This is a fairly new interpretation of the Recreational Craft Directive – European Directive 94/25-EC relating to recreational craft and is still to be tested thoroughly.

Read more on bonding on page 74

Guide: Isolation transformer

The best way to protect the boat from potentially faulty shore power is an iron-core isolation transformer. They normally weigh around 15–30 kilos or more, and may not fit easily into a smaller yacht. By using inductive (magnetic) coupling for the power supply, there is no direct connection by cables, which completely isolates the boat's AC system from the shore power.

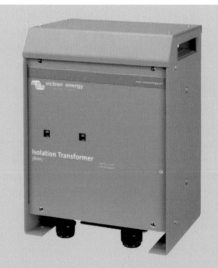

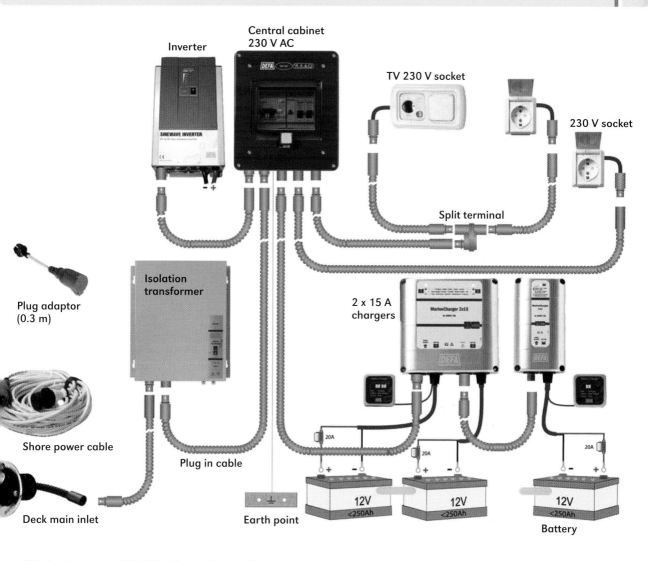

Inverter

Central cabinet
230 V AC

TV 230 V socket

230 V socket

Split terminal

Plug adaptor
(0.3 m)

Isolation
transformer

2 x 15 A
chargers

Shore power cable

Plug in cable

Deck main inlet

Earth point

12V
<250Ah

12V
<250Ah

12V
<250Ah

Battery

20A

20A

20A

This is the layout of DEFA's Plug and Play shore power system. The set-up is very similar to other systems on the market.

Right: The inlet for the shore power cable will need to be waterproof.

Bonding

According to the standard EN ISO 13297, the ground from AC shore power must be connected to the boat's ground/earth (unless using an isolation transformer). The problem is that connecting the green or green yellow ground cable from the AC shore power to metal parts in the boat may cause galvanic corrosion.

This area is much debated, and unfortunately I do not have the ultimate answer of whether to bond or not. The standard clearly states what to do, but many boat owners do not bring the shore ground onboard, but cut it at the junction box at the central cabinet.

There are two main points where leakage is prone to occur. The first is the battery chargers, which need to be of good construction with double isolation (marked with two squares, one inside the other) to ensure there is no contact between the 230 V and 12 V ground systems.

The second is a shore power water heater. This type of heater may cause problems, since it is a point where the 12 V ground system can connect with stray currents from the 230 V ground system if not correctly protected. A belt-and-braces safeguard is to take the 2- or 3-pin plug out of the socket whenever the heater is not being used.

A solution is to have a separate ground plate outside the boat for the AC ground. The ground cable should connect through the hull – this means drilling a hole – and be connected to a copper plate roughly the size of A5 paper (148 x 210 mm). The sintered plates commonly used for short wave radios are not necessary – you can use normal copper plate. The plate can be bonded with one component PU adhesive directly on to the hull, for instance in front of the rudder, where there are already disturbances in the water flow.

There is so much more to be said about this, but further detail is beyond the scope of this book.

A proper grounded system should have all parts connected and a plate on the outside of the hull.

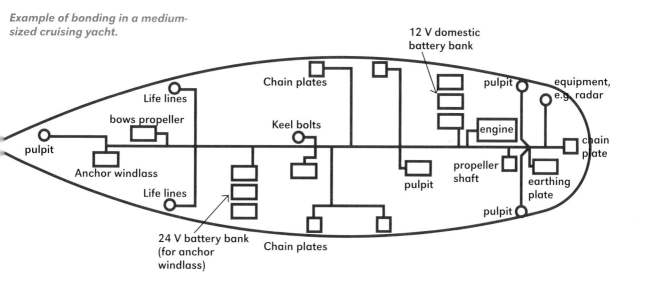

Example of bonding in a medium-sized cruising yacht.

Terminology on board

Circuit breaker (CB). A mechanical switching device to protect from short circuit or overload.

Galvanic corrosion. An electrochemical process in which one metal corrodes preferentially to another when both metals are in electrical contact and immersed in an electrolyte.

Ground or earth. In AC-powered equipment, exposed metal parts are connected to earth to prevent contact with a dangerous voltage if electrical insulation fails.

EN ISO 13297. This International Standard specifies the requirements for the design, construction and installation of low-voltage AC electrical systems that operate at nominal voltages of less than 250 V single phase on small craft of hull length up to 24 m.

Residual Current Device (RCD). Also called a ground-fault circuit interrupter. Electromechanical switching device, designed to break currents when the residual current attains a given value under specified conditions.

Sacrificial anode. An electropositive metal, most commonly zinc, connected to form a galvanic cell that protects a (more important) electronegative metal from corrosion.

Zinc saver. Also known as a galvanic isolator. A solution to give better, even if not total, protection against stray currents that will cause galvanic corrosion. Installed in series with the AC shore-power cable to block low-voltage DC galvanic current flow. Cheaper than an isolation transformer and hence more popular.

Project: Install a plug and play system

PROJECT FACTS

DIFFICULTY: easy

TIME: 3 hours

MATERIAL: A ready-made kit with everything included; extension cord, inlet, plug 'n' play cables, chargers etc.

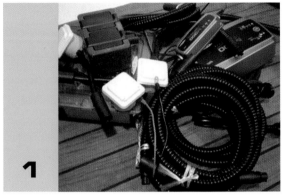

▲ The system is delivered by post in a couple of boxes including both shore power plug 'n' play parts and two chargers.

▲ A 70 mm hole saw was used inside the cockpit coaming to protect it from weather and from being accidentally stepped on.

▲ The stainless steel inlet (IP65) was screwed in place and connected to an extension cable (max 3 m).

▲ The cable is run through to the interior and fixed in place at 30 cm intervals.

The central electrical cabinet is waterprotected but should still be placed somewhere protected, and preferably close to the inlet.

6

▲ Outlets are installed in a couple of places for when direct use is desirable – most often to charge mobile phones and the computer.

7

▲ An inboard 230 V outlet is connected directly from the electrical cabinet and is RCD protected.

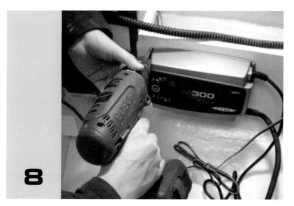

8

▲ Included in the shore power kit were two chargers. A 25 A one for the consumer battery bank...

9

▲ ... and a smaller charger for the started battery (see Chapter 4). Installation complete.

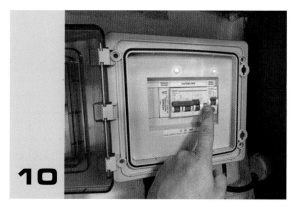

10

▲ Always test the Residual Current Device by its test button directly after plugging in the shore power.

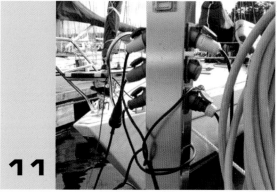

11

▲ To find a free outlet on the dock is more often than not quite difficult. Normally they are 6 or 10 A and not suitable for sharing between two boats.

07
THE DISTRIBUTION PANEL

THE DISTRIBUTION PANEL

Even for a novice, it can be quite easy to see when the old distribution panel needs replacing. It is common to find some oxidation on switches and connectors, especially connector surfaces on the fuses (which have to be turned and twisted to remove surface corrosion), unmistakable signs that it is time to get a new one.

You can find a suitable, good-quality distribution panel in a specialist equipment shop, or possibly online if you have already done your research and know exactly what you want.

If you choose the very cheapest panel, you must consider that the operation may not be reliable after a few years, due to corrosion and substandard components. The quality of a more expensive panel is normally better, but it will cost considerably more.

As always, you have to identify the products that do the job at the most reasonable cost.

That is mainly why I chose to build my own control panel...

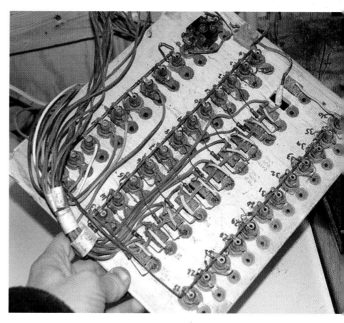

The old panel from 1977 in Roobarb had long ago seen its best days. I did not even try and identify the functions or where the mainly unmarked cables ran.

FOCUS DISTRIBUTION PANELS

Two cheap panels that, unfortunately, often are sold by chandlers. If you update your system, I strongly suggest you go for better quality. It will pay for it self in the long run.

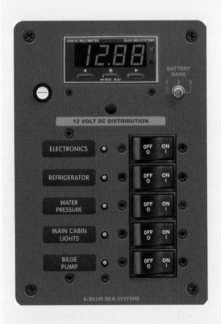

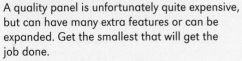

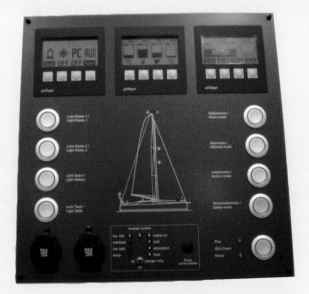

A quality panel is unfortunately quite expensive, but can have many extra features or can be expanded. Get the smallest that will get the job done.

MAKING A PANEL

No boat's system is identical, and by making your own panel you get exactly what you need.

Although I chose to make my own control panel for *Roobarb*, I utilized standard components. I designed the panel to fit A3 paper size (the standard format for the laser etching company I used), using a drawing programme with vector graphics. The best known are probably CorelDRAW and Adobe Illustrator; a CAD programme can also do the job, but they cost a lot of money.

For a cheaper option, you can download a program like Inkscape or DrawPlus from the internet for free and try them out.

Using a vector graphics program can often be a steep learning curve, and you may be better off getting help from someone who is already familiar with it.

I also inserted a simplified image of *Roobarb* with LEDs in position to indicate when different navigations lights were in use. When I was happy with the result, I emailed the file to a company that makes laser engravings and cut-outs, which I had found on the internet. There are many small sign-making businesses that do laser engravings combined with laser cutting. Try the Yellow Pages for your area or look online.

With the help of a friendly electrical expert, I then bought components from the internet and put them together to make a panel for a fraction of the price of one from the specialist.

There were many switches and thus many cables fighting for space behind the panel, and cable ties were used in abundance.

The drawback with my own panel was that the size was quite large, as were my chosen components.

As with other elements of the project, the trickiest part was how to use the available space. In a 27-footer it is rather limited.

The easiest solution is just to buy a panel off the shelf. But when getting a quality one it will be quite expensive.

Economy was not what made me make my own, but rather available space and the number of switches I thought I needed (turned out to be too many).

I tried to make the design simple and use the commonest size, 12 millimetre, for the cutout for the switches. Everything that is to be cut out should have a special colour. I chose red to make it stand out against the black lines that were to be engraved in the fake brushed aluminium surface.

The plastic was not very rigid, but I glued it (it already had self-adhesive on the back) to a stiffer panel before making a frame of oak and screwing it into place.

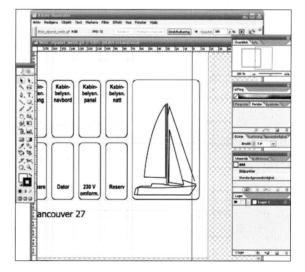

Project: Install a distribution panel

PROJECT FACTS

DIFFICULTY: easy

TIME: approx. 8 hours including building the oak frame

COST: About £20 for the laser engraving of the panel. Switches and fuses around £80. Cost of cables etc are included in other projects.

TOOLS: An illustration program to make the design.

▲ The old panel and cables were long overdue for replacement. The easiest way was to rip it all out and start from scratch.

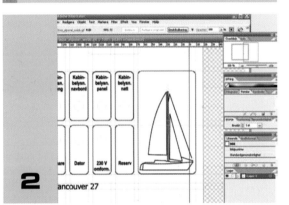

▲ My home-designed panel was created in an illustration programme and then sent off to be laser-cut. Many businesses have a laser-engraving machine, which can often also do light cutting in plastic panels.

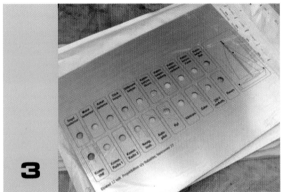

▲ A few days later the panel was returned by post and the work could continue.

▲ The new panel was fitted with stainless toggle switches. These switches are fairly cheap and damp-proof.

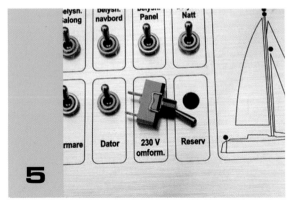

▲ I made many separate switches to cater for many consumers. Maybe too many, as I didn't use them all in the end...

▲ All cables were bundled in ties and secured at the back of the panel.

▲ I made a frame out of oak for the panel, to form a neat unit that could be attached to the bulkhead under the bridge deck.

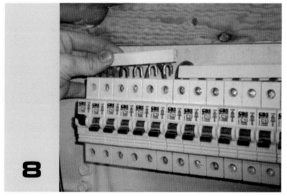

▲ Plain domestic automatic circuit breakers for AC-voltage were fitted between the panel and the positive terminal block. A common positive cable from the consumer bank was then linked to all the fuses.

▲ Then the task of connecting all the circuits began – a few days of intensive labour.

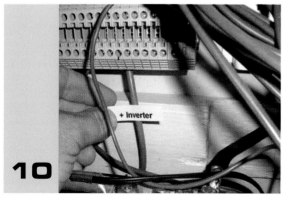

▲ The very important task of marking every cable should not be left to the end. Do it as you go along.

▲ The first test went well. To finish, all the loose cables around the cabinet need to be tidied up.

08

THE INVERTER

THE INVERTER

**Not too long ago, almost all the equipment you used on board
ran just fine from paraffin, and later from the onboard battery.
But this is no longer the case. Now we want the convenience of
230 volt on board.**

An inverter converts a 12 V DC supply to 240 V AC
which, provided the inverter is rated for the power
required, in theory allows you to plug in any mains-
powered device you might use at home – hairdryer,
mobile phone charger or even a microwave oven, for
instance. Almost all you have to do is plug it in.

However, you need to be aware that some items
of 240 V equipment draw a lot of current, so it's
important to take the battery capacity into account.
A simple 1000 W (1 kW) hairdryer uses up a 100 Ah
battery bank in just over half an hour.

Hairdryers and vacuum cleaners are the particular
household devices that drain the batteries, so if you
use these at sea, the whole electrical system must be
sized accordingly, resulting in higher costs.

Needless to say, to have an inverter on board
is far from necessary for all leisure boats – most
are perfectly fine with a 12 V charger, or a DC-DC
converter (more about this later), thereby making a
considerable saving.

When possible, try to use the inverter only when
you are charging from the running engine.

SINE OR SQUARE WAVE

There are two ways in which an inverter can make DC
voltage, and it may be important to make the right
choice if you have sensitive equipment that you want
to run at 240 V.

The cheapest and commonest inverter, which is
widely available at hypermarkets, petrol stations and
on the shelves of chandlers, is the one with a modified
sine wave (i.e. a square wave).

Without too many theoretical details about how
DC voltage works, you could say that this type of
inverter gives a less clean voltage, which may possibly
create problems if you are using sensitive electrical
equipment, such as some computers, fluorescent
tubes and motors in vacuum cleaners or refrigerators.

Many experts claim that it makes no difference,
and that most products can withstand a modified
square wave. Inverters with a modified sine wave are
available from about £25–30.

But if you want to be on the safe side, you buy a
somewhat more expensive inverter, which converts
the 12 V into a real sine wave. It means a cleaner
voltage and more complex electronics – and therefore
it is much more expensive, around £150 for a 300 W
model.

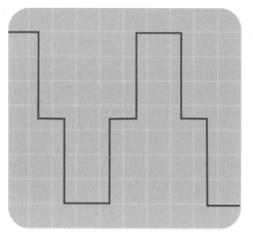 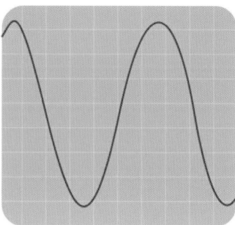

The difference between a modified wave and a pure sine wave can be clearly seen in an oscilloscope (a graphic view of curves). The former is cheaper and works for most equipment on board.

CHOOSING AN INVERTER

Calculating the size of the inverter should be based on the heaviest load (which can be substantial at the moment of start-up) on the equipment that you connect.

Of course, the simplest thing is to buy the largest possible inverter, but then you are talking several hundred pounds, and a rather big metal box that needs to be installed in a well-ventilated spot on the boat. There are inverters for leisure boats that can tolerate 3000 W or more.

I opted for a smaller inverter, and therefore I have to wait until I reach a harbour with shore power to use any power-intensive electric tools (such as my angle grinder) or other high consumers.

I bought a 300 W inverter that can handle a monitor and a small computer with a total of approximately 120 W.

Most inverters can handle a higher power output for a few seconds without blowing a fuse.

Terminology onboard

AC-DC: AC stands for alternating current (so-called 220 V, normally 230–240 V), and DC stands for direct current and is continuous voltage (so called 12 V, normally 12.5–13.5 V).

Voltage converter: turns one continuous voltage into another, for example 24 volt to 12 volt, or can receive 9–15 V and provide consistent 12 V output voltage. Some converters available let you choose the output voltage, for example

15/16/18/19 or 24 volt. These are perfect for running a laptop with minimal loss, rather than convert the 12 V in the battery into 240 V and then back to 14–19 V, which most laptops use.

Inverter: electronically transforms 12 V DC to 240 V AC, for powering equipment that cannot be run on 12 V. In simple terms, you could say it works like an inverse battery charger.

CONVERSION EFFICIENCY

The conversion efficiency tells you how efficiently a system converts energy into practical work in some form. A modern inverter has a conversion efficiency of more than 90 per cent – that is, the loss when you convert 12 V to 240 V is relatively small.

However, an inverter does consume power even when nothing is switched on. The consumption for an idle inverter can be as much as 3–5 W, so if you leave the boat for a couple of weeks, the battery may be empty on your return. You should therefore switch off the inverter's own power switch, unless the whole power system is switched off by a main switch (which it normally should be).

DC-DC CONVERTER

If you only have one or two devices to power or charge, a good solution is often a small DC-DC converter. It converts the 12 V to the 3, 5 or 18 V your device needs.

If charging small batteries for mobile phones etc is what you need most, then it may be best to purchase the (often) fairly cheap dedicated chargers that plug into a lighter socket. These are available for mobile phones, MP3 players and other small devices with batteries.

A laptop normally runs on a voltage of 15–20 V (check the power supply unit or the manual for details). There are small converters that turn the 12 V from batteries into various voltages, and they cost around £25. The one I bought for £22 runs the computer straight from the boat's batteries. Read more about converters in the box on this page.

During all transfer of voltage, some is lost in the conversion. DC voltage to AC and back to DC again loses a few per cent.

I have both options (inverter and DC-DC converter) and I have noticed that the DC-DC converter on its own has a lower consumption, compared to when the inverter runs the computer. Not by much, but after a few hours it all adds up.

A friend tested one of his laptops and found a difference of up to 0.4 A (1.4 A when the computer is charging) between running the computer through the DC converter and a sine wave converter with AC voltage.

I bought a small universal voltage converter for power supply and charging for the laptop (and other equipment) straight from the boat's batteries. The same converter can also be used in some aircraft, if you want to work during a long-haul flight.

The output voltage is adapted with the use of an exchangeable clamp (15, 16, 17, 18, 19 or 24 V) and the plug is inserted into a lighter socket. At the other end, there is a collection of plugs to fit the computer's power socket, which of course looks different on different computers. Maximum continuous power output is 72 W.

An expert friend also recommended that – if possible – you check that the converter is galvanically isolated, so that the input negative has no contact with the output negative.

Laptop consumption varies, depending on whether the computer's battery is charged or not, how much of the hard disk is running, and if a DVD player is in use. Mine used 3.5 A normally, but up to 5 A when charging the battery and I was using the digital chart programme.

The installation of the inverter was to find a space behind the panel and use four stainless screws. 6mm² cables connected the unit to the busbars in the panel.

Inverters at a glance

A common problem with inverters is that they cut out when the voltage in the battery bank is too low, often as a result of the batteries not having received enough charge, according to expert Herman Beijerbergen.

He stresses the importance of sizing the batteries to suit the estimated effect you want from the inverter.

This will prevent an excessive voltage dip at the start-up of power-intensive devices such as hairdryers, microwaves and vacuum cleaners. If a hairdryer is rated 1500 W, it can consume twice that power during the first second or so. However, most inverters handle this fairly well.

Remember that many consumers (such as cookers, kettles or vacuum cleaners) have a starting current that can be up to two or three times the rating on the device.

A compressor in a refrigerator or air-conditioning unit can consume up to 20 times the rating during start-up. Calculate the size of the inverter according to your needs.

OTHER PROBLEMS

The term 'ripple' can be described as 'alternating current in the direct current' in the cables going into the inverter, which cannot handle it very well. All inverters have some problem with ripple effect and this can cause the inverter to cut out at a much lower load than its stated tolerance. Shorter and larger cables can be a solution.

My expert friend also says that the more sophisticated the electronics, the more important it is to choose an inverter with a pure sine wave. However, he adds that most computers can tolerate an inverter with a modified wave, but that electric motors often need a good sine wave to work properly.

The primary signs of this are that machines get 'tired' and generate poor output.

TOP 5 TIPS

1. Ensure that the intended installation position for the inverter has adequate ventilation – if not, the conversion efficiency is significantly reduced, or the inverter will cut out when it overheats.

2. Ensure that the cables are large enough – it is preferable to use one size up from the manufacturer's table (ratio between cable diameter and length) of specifications.

3. Position the inverter as close to the battery bank as possible.

4. Monitor power consumption – using a hairdryer and a kettle simultaneously requires a large inverter.

5. Adapt the capacity of the inverter to the estimated needs – maybe a bigger size than planned is already necessary...

The generator

Another way to get AC on board (and DC for that matter) is to install a separate generator that will take the strain off the main engine just for producing electricity for onboard demand.

The fuel is most often diesel, but there are small transportable generators fueled by petrol/gasoline and may be brought out when extra power is needed – say to run electrical power tools for a repair somewhere remote.

The large diesel generator is for boats larger than 40 foot, but the small portable one can be a backup for any boat.

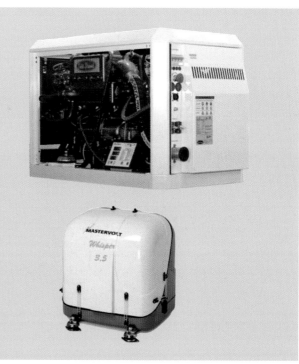

09

LIGHTING

>> INTERIOR LIGHTING

Boat interiors need good lighting; however, the lights often end up being the biggest power consumers on board.

My rationale is that several small lamps are better than a few large ones, as it is easier to adjust the light and thereby save power by only using the lamps needed at the time.

12 V light bulbs are gradually disappearing from the chandlers and even halogen bulbs are becoming less popular; now it is basically all about LED. The good news is that LEDs use very little power. The bad news is that most have a fairly low light yield (and high yield LEDs are expensive).

This means that, in each lamp, you put together 5–20 LEDs in a cluster, for better light distribution.

Now there are also warm-white LEDs, which are increasingly replacing the cold and less cosy blue-white. The warm-white ones are still a bit more expensive, and if you buy a cheap light fitting you will no doubt get cold-white LEDs. If this matters to you, check before buying.

CHOOSING LIGHTS

What lights you choose mainly depends on what you want to spend. If you already have good lights with ordinary light bulbs or halogen bulbs, and you are happy, you can obviously keep them. Then you just supplement wherever necessary.

If all the lighting needs replacing, the best solution, in my opinion, is to use energy-efficient LEDs.

Remember that light distribution is often poor,

especially with cheap LED lights, and you may therefore need several to illuminate the same area as a halogen or ordinary light bulb.

I also chose to install light strips along the cabin sides, to throw some light into the corners for a much nicer ambience, and they are left on for a couple of hours each night. These light strips turned out to be the most used, since the indirect warm light made the cabin cosy and the hidden placement under the deck was unobtrusive.

You do not have to change the whole fitting for the lamp. There are replacement 'bulbs' that are LEDs that will fit your old lamp.

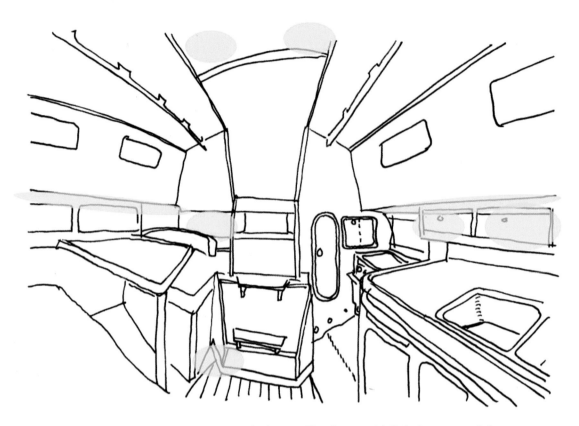

If more light is needed during shorter periods, for example for reading, halogen bulbs may be the best option. When I bought my iPad, bedtime reading became easier with the backlit screen – now I read all books and most magazines this way.

FITTING THE LIGHTS

When fitting the lights, it was important to arrange them in logical clusters for the cable connection from the control panel. I grouped them in boat areas: cabin, galley, sleeping area, forepeak and on deck (i.e. deck and cockpit lighting).

Then I arranged each area individually, and gave the six halogen spotlights (6 x 5 W) set in the deckhead their own switch/dimmer, so there is no need to have the lights on full, which saves energy. The large deckhead lamp for ambient light has its own switch on the lamp itself.

In the sleeping area there are both overhead lights and reading lights next to the bunks, with their own switches. In the forepeak on *Roobarb*, where there is nothing but the toilet and storage space, there are

The theory with light is to spread the sources to create an adjustable mix – from working light when cooking to ambient lights later at night. In the ceiling there are six halogen spotlights, which can be dimmed.

Under the deck there are tube lights with LEDs that give an excellent ambient light and also lighten those often dark corners. Small red LEDs make it possible to move around safely when night sailing.

Above the galley there is an effective LED strip light that uses only 4 W but gives ample lighting.

Right: This was the small dinette after remodelling (see Upgrading your Boat's Interior, *published by Adlard Coles Nautical). I added an LED string light under the side deck and dimmable spotlights in the deckheadf.*

The lights in the cabin are rather muted, with a spotlight in the deckhead and a bedside reading lamp with a halogen bulb.

two large halogen light fittings, which are either on or off – their purpose is to provide good light when you are looking for something. This is no place for ambient lighting.

For the galley I used lighting in the shape of a light strip with 60 warm-white LEDs (totalling 4 W), providing

an even light along the whole workbench, which is about a metre long. For everyday tasks, such as cutting and chopping, good lighting is required. I still have not found a lamp that I like for above the dining table, so maybe I will make one myself – I have made rough sketches for a waterproof LED crystal chandelier.

In the galley, the many small sources of light make it easy to adjust to suit the task.

Project: Install lighting

PROJECT FACTS

DIFFICULTY: easy

TIME: 10 hours, spread over several occasions

MATERIAL: LED lighting is still slightly more expensive than filament or halogen-based lamps. I bought many but did not install them all.

▲ The six overhead spotlights now have a common 12 V dimmer, to create cosy lighting and save energy at the same time.

▲ The cabin deckhead spotlights provide good working light when needed. Normally smaller spotlights or small LEDs, which consume less power, are used.

▲ In the mast I installed a new floodlight for the foredeck. Easy to do when the mast was lowered.

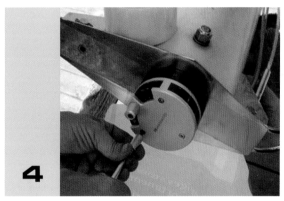

▲ In the masthead I installed one of the LED navigational lights combined with an anchor light. It will save energy compared with a traditional light during a full night's sail.

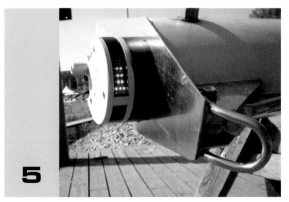

▲ A multi-LED navigation light was mounted in the masthead. This will help to save a lot of power during dark nights.

▲ To let the cables pass through the cabintop roof, I installed a waterproof box in stainless steel.

10
SUN

CHARGING FROM THE SUN

The free energy source of the sun makes it smart to include a few solar panels to keep your batteries happy.

A soft solar panel is perfect for mounting on the boom cover, to trickle-charge the batteries when the boat is moored in the home harbour, without using shore power.

A hard panel can either be rigid with a tempered glass front, or be a little flexible, with a stainless or aluminium plate on the back, and can be manipulated to fit around a curve, for example on a hatch coaming. It is strong enough to tread on occasionally.

SOLAR PANELS

In my view, it is a top priority to make use of the sun's energy on board a cruising boat. One or more solar cells normally provide the best energy return per each pound invested, and two 25 W panels can produce up to 25 Ah of additional charging current per day in the West Indies. In Swedish waters, it may only be half of this on a sunny day. But it is still a good supplement, which means you do not have to run the engine as often just to charge the batteries, or find a guest harbour with shore power.

For *Roobarb* I bought two 24 W cells from the Finnish company Naps, which I fixed to the struts of the new stainless pipe frame (for the mainsheet) with the use of ready-made adjustable brackets from the Swedish firm Noa. These brackets, which were actually quite expensive (about £70), made it a very easy task and are the only choice if you have ordinary 25 mm tubes.

The alternative to fitting them in that position would have been on the pushpit or on deck or the hatch coaming (which I tried first). The two latter options offer no possibility of turning the solar cells perpendicular to the sun for optimal effect. Of course, you may not want to stay on board all day just to turn the panels to the sun, in which case a 'flat' installation can be a good compromise. In reality there are not usually that many suitable places on board, so the panels have to be fitted where there is space.

A stainless radar arch at the stern or a rotating post are other good options.

REGULATOR

A regulator protects against overcharging

The voltage from a solar panel is usually higher than the 12.75 V in the battery bank, often around 18–20 V.

Therefore the voltage must be regulated to the correct level to prevent the battery from being overcharged (when no load is applied). A regulator also stops the current from 'going backwards' at night through an integrated blocking diode.

There is a surprisingly large number of regulators

on the market, with more or less sophisticated features. Some can control the charge from several sources. I have a separate battery meter, so I opted for the simplest one.

INSTALLATION

All solar cells need some kind of regulator, as the voltage can be very high (21 V when I tested it). The battery current can also 'escape' through the back of the solar panels at night. I got Naps' own regulator, Mmobile, where you can connect several panels in parallel and then on to the batteries. Actually, the leads from the regulator should also be connected directly to the battery terminals, if you read the instructions. I settled for connecting them over a 10 A automatic fuse to the terminal via the control panel, which in turn is connected to the batteries with a 35 mm^2 large tin-plated cable.

The actual task of connecting the panels was not a problem but, as is so often the case, it was the planning and, above all, where to put the panels that took up most of the project time. I wanted to be able to angle the panels according to the position of the sun, at the same time as preventing strong winds or high waves from sweeping them away. I was also aware that the slightest shadow, even from a shroud, would reduce the panel effectiveness significantly. Realizing that this could not be avoided altogether, I

figured out that a compromise where the panels were placed on top of the spray hood would work best.

Noa's aluminium brackets facilitated the installation, as well as a mast base made of composite boards. The cables were pulled through a hole in the deck just under the arch for the mainsheet system.

SAVING ENERGY

Being conservative with what you use on board saves a lot of battery capacity, with the result that you do not need to charge as often. Most of the power onboard *Roobarb* is consumed by the refrigerator, followed by the lighting and the (navigation) computer, when it is running.

To keep all fresh food cold I installed a modern refrigerator with a water-cooled condenser from Isotherm. I also used twice the recommended thickness of insulation – the material is ground insulation boards made out of extruded polystyrene, which provide the best insulation for the price.

The lighting is divided between many small lamps, as I believe that lighting adapted to suit the task (cooking, cleaning the boat, or sitting in the reading corner with a good book) keeps down consumption. Many lamps are also LEDs, which use very little power. In the saloon deckhead there are six halogen spotlights with a dimmer that makes it easy to adjust the light level.

Project: Install solar panels

PROJECT FACTS

DIFFICULTY: easy

TIME: 2 hours

MATERIAL: Depends on method of panel installation; either glue, or the adjustable brackets I used here.

1

 I bought the panels by mail order – two small 24 W panels sized to fit somewhere on my rather small boat.

▲ First of all, I needed to find the right place for the panels. The hatch cover was good, but the angling potential on the struts of the new mainsheet frame was better.

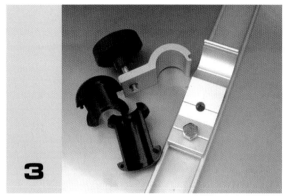

▲ When I had settled for the frame, I bought ready-made adjustable brackets from a specialist.

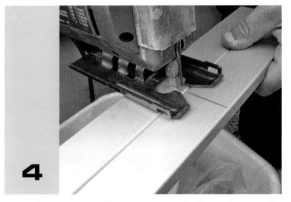

▲ Aluminium profiles were cut to fit the rather small solar panels. They protrude by 1 cm or so to provide protection in strong winds.

▲ The brackets were attached to the 25 mm pipe and secured with a stainless bolt.

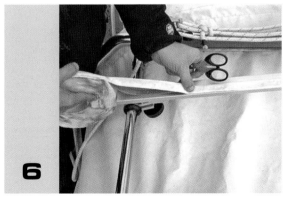

▲ To reduce corrosion between the aluminium and stainless steel, a strip of butyl rubber was placed between the panel and the bracket.

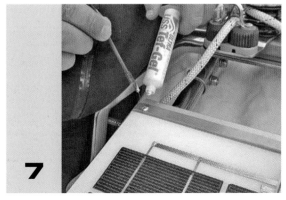

▲ In all the holes where screws would be inserted, we used a little Tef-Gel to form a barrier against corrosion.

8

▲ Then it just remained to tighten all the screws. The butyl rubber strip is also adhesive and holds the panels in place.

9

▲ Now that both panels are mounted on top of the spray hood, I hope they will be out of harm's way and also catch as much sun as possible.

10

▲ The cable was attached along the mainsheet frame with ordinary bundling cable ties, and a waterproof connector then led the cables to the inside of the boat.

11

▲ We tested to see if it worked, and it sure did! Almost 21 V (unloaded) with a thin veil of hazy clouds.

12

A regulator placed behind the distribution panel close to the busbars brings down the charge voltage to 14.2–15.5 V.

13

▲ All cables were bundled and led into the regulator. Here you can also see the cables with jointing sleeves connected in parallel.

GUIDE: Solar panels

Solar panels are divided into two categories: hard and soft. Soft ones are cheaper and can be attached temporarily to a boom cover with rubber cords to take care of trickle charge when you are not on the boat.

Hard ones are almost always stationary and designed to be fixed to the boat, typically to the cabin roof or the targa arch frame. They can be slippery to walk on. One type has an aluminium frame and a glass surface.

The largest individual solar cells suitable for marine use are about 100–130 W. Those are just over 1 m² in size and weigh around 10 kg, with a glass front and aluminium frame. Soft thin-film panels are often a little smaller, usually around 15–30 W, weighing 1–2 kg.

Sometimes marine panels are mentioned, which have a stainless (or aluminium) backing plate that makes the back of the panel semi-rigid, and a laminated plastic cover over the cells, which make them more resistant to salt water and to being trodden on occasionally.

The most critical thing is to avoid all shade on the panels, as the tiniest shroud is enough to reduce the charging voltage drastically. They should preferably also be positioned perpendicular to the sun.

+ Provide a lot of energy return for each invested pound during their lifetime

+ Maintenance free, in principle

- The tiniest shadow reduces charge drastically.

Right: To lead the cables from the panel into the inside of the cabin, to be hooked up to charge the batteries, you need to use a waterproof through deck gland.

The flexible panel can be placed wherever you have space for it. Until now they have been less efficient and a bit more expensive than their rigid counterparts.

The hard, glassless panel with aluminium backing is probably the best on board. These have dropped sharply in price the last couple of years.

If possible, allow your panel(s) to swing to face the sun at right angles.

11

WIND POWER

>> WIND POWER

They say that the wind is free. That is true, but wind turbines suited to boats are far from free!

A wind generator is good to have, for example, in the West Indies, where there is a constant and continuous trade wind blowing. The drawback, however, is that you tend to moor in a well-protected spot, which is not conducive to power generation. And you often sail across the seas with the wind at your back, which means little power from a wind turbine.

There are some smaller, easily powered generators that produce low current that is perfect for trickle-charging a battery bank when the boat is moored at home.

I read several reviews before I bought the new Air Breeze, which in Sweden is only sold in the shore version (different type of paint on the aluminium case). I ordered my marine version directly from the US, and saved a couple of hundred pounds.

Air Breeze is a successor to the Air-X, which is common on long-distance sailing boats. Air-X has a reputation for requiring a gale to be able to charge fully and for keeping boat neighbours moored nearby awake at night with its noisy 'fluttering' as it gathers speed with the wind gusts.

However, Air Breeze claims to have improved rotor blades and to be able to start charging at a wind speed of 7 knots. The graph from the manufacturer says it will charge up to 16 A (approximately 200 W) at 25 knots.

A wind generator will work on overcast days, but when sailing downwind the apparent wind speed may not be enough to start the charging. Some turbines are very noisy - check the feedback from current owners. This is the Air Breeze I bought for **Roobarb.**

There is an integrated regulator in the generator housing and an electronic overcharge protection that makes the rotor slow down when the wind is too strong. Preferably, there should also be a circuit breaker that disconnects and slows down the wind turbine when the wind is very strong, for example. A 50 A fuse should also be included in the installation.

GUIDE: Wind generators

A wind generator does not have a propeller, but a rotor. No practical difference, I guess.

There are about 10–15 products on the market designed or suitable for leisure boats. KISS and Air-X are two types that long-distance sailors have opted for.

+ Wind is free

+ Provides a lot of charge when the wind blows

− Can be noisy

− Expensive.

A small wind generator may be used to trickle charge the batteries, when in port with no possibility of hooking up to shore power.

New models are released onto the market all the time. Make sure you do your homework on what current model of wind generator is the quietest and gives best amperage in low winds.

Project: **Install a wind generator**

PROJECT FACTS

DIFFICULTY: Easy

TIME: 2 hours

COST: The wind generator cost about £600 when imported. The pole and supports where about £50.

TOOLS: None, apart from the normal toolbox.

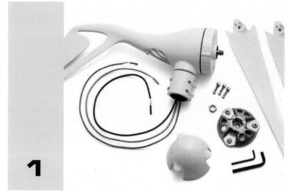

1

▲ The wind generator was supplied in sections that needed assembling.

2

▲ I made the pole from a stainless tube, having measured that I could stand on the side of the coaming to the cockpit under the generator without getting an unscheduled haircut.

3

▲ On the dock in Caernarfon I hacksawed the pole as there was no electricity.

4

▲ The generator head came with some rubber to isolate it and reduce vibrations reverberating in the hull.

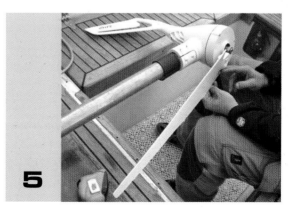

5

▲ The actual assembly was quite straightforward and gave few problems.

12
THE MOTORBOAT

A NEW SYSTEM IN THE MOTORBOAT

In another project boat, a motorboat from the early 1980s, I wanted a compact and simplified electrical system. But even though I aimed for simple, there was more work than I first expected.

The condition of the 5-metre project boat, bought especially for a series of articles, was a lot worse than I had hoped for. But then the Delta 17HT, from the mid 1980s, only cost us £500 so maybe I shouldn't have expected much else.

The electrical system was appalling, but nothing was to be kept for the rebuild. Corroded cables and obsolete electronics were all going to be replaced. My journalist colleague, Lars, and I wanted to see how little could be done for a functional system. Two batteries, one 70 Ah starter battery and one bigger 110 Ah consumer battery, would serve the interior lighting, navigation lights, a chart plotter, a small refrigerator, a tank meter and a fuel flow meter to check the fuel consumption; as in a car, this would tell us the optimal speed for best mileage. Simplicity would be the word, and we wanted a system that would work for the next 10–15 years.

CHOOSING MATERIAL
We also wanted a new, effective alternator for the boat – this can make a big difference when it comes to charging the batteries, especially if you are keeping an older inboard engine. We calculated that charging from the engine is sufficient on a motorboat, since the engine is normally run for a couple of hours every day

when out on a boating holiday. A portable charger would be brought onto the boat whenever necessary, but we would not install a separate shore power system.

We found that, as in my sailing boat, space was at a premium. The best available space was under the floorboards, as here the batteries would be low and centred. The drawback would be if the boat were to fill with a lot of water – a broken bilge pump or some heavy rain, for instance, could wreck the equipment. But all in all, this was the best position we could find for the batteries and some of the other equipment.

Even though we were trying to keep the cost down, we did not want to buy substandard material – a few hundred pounds would be pretty insignificant in a project like this, and we wanted reliable material that wouldn't leave us high and dry. Money could be saved elsewhere in the renovation, but not on the electrical system.

Therefore we used material from well-known manufacturers, among them BEP and Blue Sea. All cables were tin-plated, as they are only marginally more expensive if bought from the more trusted sources. We chose to install standard open-cell lead batteries as they provide sufficient length of service, and this boat is used in protected waters and close to service if needed.

As with *Roobarb*, we started to calculate the power consumption. The correct battery size to buy is neither too small nor too big, as this will increase the cost. We estimated that on average we would use about 34 Ah per 24 hours at anchor.

CHARGING

The difference between a sailboat and a motorboat is that when the motorboat is in use, it will always top up the battery banks, and this avoids the damaging deep discharge of the consumer battery.

During a boating holiday, when the engine is only in use for the short periods of time it takes to get from point A to point B, the batteries will probably only be charged to 85 per cent, since in practice the last few per cent takes a long time to charge with the engine's alternator. This can be bettered when hooked up to shore power in a marina or with a large solar panel that will keep on charging.

In our case we will only have about 95 Ah (out of the marked capacity on the consumer battery of 110 Ah). Since we always try not to deep discharge the batteries below 50 per cent capacity, which for our battery is 55 Ah, the usable span is 95–55 Ah = 40 Ah. This covers the estimated 34 Ah per 24 hours, and then some.

To keep track, we have a simple battery meter installed directly on the consumer battery – the starter battery is always fully charged and has less need to be monitored. The meter is the small 'battery bug' (from Argus Analyzers) with a built-in microprocessor that displays the percentage of life remaining as well as the voltage.

BATTERY SEPARATION

To enable us to separate the starter from the consumer battery, we installed a split charger (battery separator) to ensure that the starter battery is always topped up before the engine's alternator starts charging the consumer bank (or single large battery, in our case).

The split charger detects when the voltage on the first battery reaches a predetermined level (around 13 V) and then redirects the charging to the other battery. Normally, the start battery is charged first, then the consumer bank.

This is the normal set-up, to ensure the engine always has a fully charged starter battery to enable you to get home. But I learned that it might be better to do it the other way around, and we may change the set-up to reflect this.

Normally you can combine the two banks with a switch to get the full capacity from both banks when required to start the engine and the starter battery has gone flat. Or have a split charger to take care of the consumer bank first when charging from shore power...

Spreadsheet – X3's DC load calculation				
Consumer	Watt	Ampere	Hours at anchor	Total Ah at anchor
Navigation lights	4.9	0.38	0	0
Anchor light	2.1	0.16	10	1.6
Bow flood lights	110	8.62	0	0
Interior light	40	3.13	3	9.39
Stern lights (underwater)		3.5	0	0
Cool box	33	2.58	3	7.74
Plotter/computer		5	3	15
Total				33.73
Calculated voltage in battery 12.75 V				

BIGGER ALTERNATOR

The engine is an old petrol inboard, a Volvo Penta AQ170C that was completely overhauled, and painted gold, in this project.

The original alternator was only 38 A, and one of the first upgrades we decided on was to get a new, bigger alternator of 75 A to improve charging when running under engine. We needed to modify the bracket on the engine, but this was not too tricky.

Project:
Replace an electrical system

PROJECT FACTS

DIFFICULTY: easy to medium

TIME: approx 30 hours

COST: Batteries (70 + 110 Ah) £300, tin-plated starter cable (35 mm^2) 6.5 metres at about £8/metre, tin-plated cable by the reel 4.5 mm^2 at £1/metre + 1.5/3.5 mm^2, split charger £120, fuse holder + fuses £50, panel £120, light (6 LED) £75, navigation light £140, lugs/brackets/etc approx £60.

▲ The old system was not a pretty sight when we bought the boat. A mess of corroded cables of indeterminate use – we decided to scrap everything.

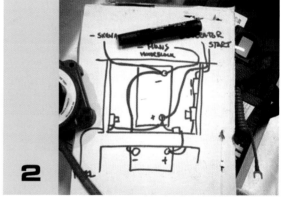

▲ We made a simple plan of how to connect everything, which saved time later on.

▲ We also needed to calculate all the cable dimensions according to power consumption. We used a computer app for this.

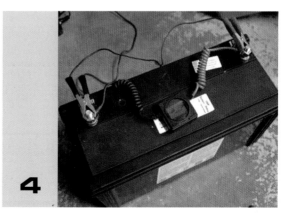

▲ For this project we used open cell lead-acid batteries for this project as they are good value for money. We began by charging them from the mains.

5

▲ The heavy batteries need substantial support in a motorboat. We used softwood timber and strong straps.

6

▲ The 35 mm² cable is measured and stripped of its rubber sheath – this can be done with a special tool or just a sharp knife.

7

The heavy duty lugs are crimped with a quality tool for a perfect airtight connection.

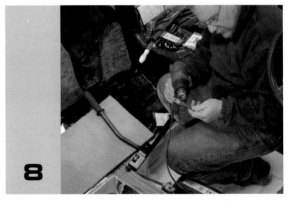

8

▲ All crimps are protected with heat shrink tubing. We used red and black tubes to make it easy to distinguish the negative and positive sides.

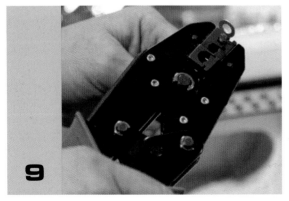

9

▲ The thinner cables were also properly crimped and given heat shrink covers.

10

▲ The starter battery was given an in-line 50 A fuse.

▲ The consumer battery was given a separate 150 A fuse, placed as close as possible to the battery. The cover is to protect against sparks.

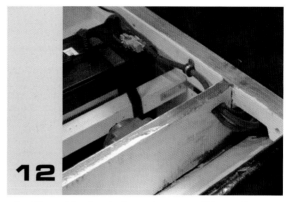

▲ The cables for the batteries were all 35 mm^2 and installed with P-brackets and through holes for a functional layout.

▲ The automatic charging relay separates the starter and consumer batteries.

▲ The negative (–) side was bonded to the engine, which makes a common ground for the 12 V system.

▲ Almost there – the consumer battery is secured with straps and the starter one is about to be strapped down.

▲ The panel was the simplest one we could find, with only six switches and standard blade fuses integrated into it.

17

▲ On the back, all connections were made and the terminals given heat shrink covers. The cables were tinned.

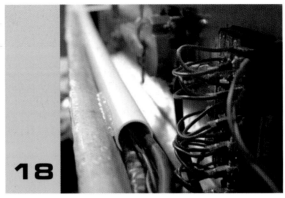

18

▲ We hot-glued a 32 mm PVC conduit pipe along the side to protect the cables and to make later additions simple.

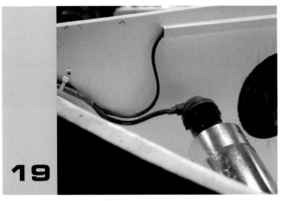

19

▲ The bow docking lights (110 W for two) have chunky cables of 4.5 mm^2 to serve the 6-metre cable run from the panel and back.

20

In the aft section we installed a busbar to serve some of the equipment in this area.

21

▲ The lighted name of the boat *X3* and two underwater lights were installed together with trim interceptors that all needed electricity.

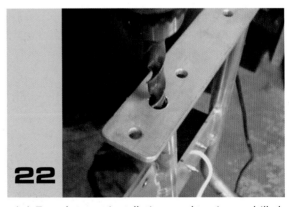

22

▲ To make some installations unobtrusive we drilled holes in the gantry to be able to run cables inside it.

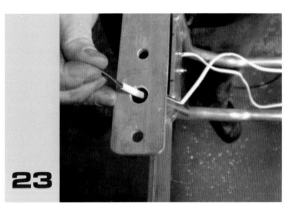

23

▲ We pulled the cables inside the piping of the gantry for the LED navigation lights and to prepare for a future radar dome and GPS antenna.

24

▲ The nav lights were served from this installation and were some of the last major work we did. Some small additions were to come later.

TIPS

1. Change everything where the currents are high – between the alternator, starter motor and the engine battery are particularly important, but the refrigerator, anchor windlass and bow thruster are also important.

2. Use large diameter cable, preferably of tin-plated copper.

3. Have more than one method of topping up the batteries, apart from the alternator – shore power or maybe solar panels.

4. The electrical system is one of the most important on board. If this fails, many other functions also fail. Use a battery meter to maintain a better overview.

5. If you have no experience in installing electrics, ask a reliable tradesman to carry out the planning and calculations. You can then install the parts according to his/her instructions.

6. Always try to make perfect crimps. Buy, borrow or rent good-quality crimpers.

7. Protect the cable ends with heat shrink tubing and Vaseline.

8. Label all cables and keep a record of what you have installed. This will save a lot of hassle a few years down the line.

9. Protect all cables from chafe by running them through plastic piping. A short cut can be expensive or possibly even dangerous if it starts a fire.

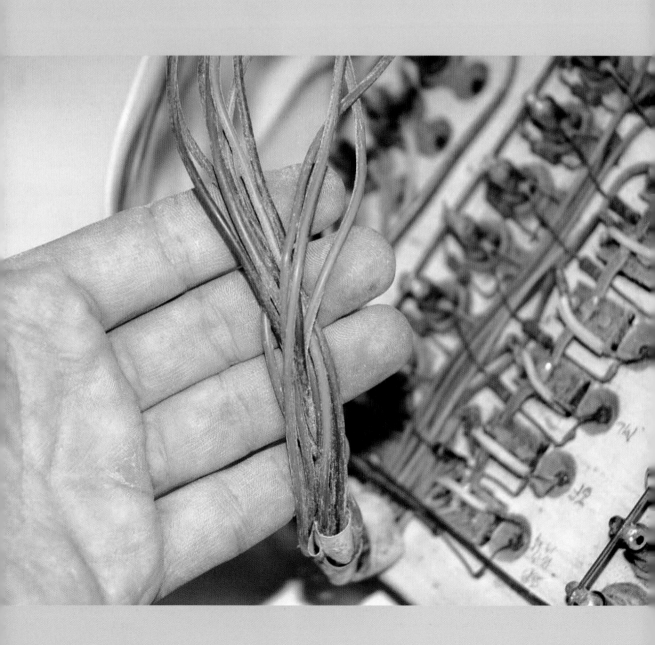

13
LESSONS

LESSONS LEARNED THE HARD WAY

To sum up all the lessons I learned from the project, I offer here a few reflections.

Basically, I knew very little about electricity on board before I started the project. I knew the difference between ampere and volt, but that was more or less the extent of my knowledge.

I talked to a lot of experts and sometimes found their advice hard to interpret – in order to understand all the terminology, you need some prior knowledge (or an engineer's degree in electronics).

I wanted to keep the project on a practical level, without too much theory. If you want to delve into theory, or to gather more in-depth information, there are many good books available, describing the process far more clearly than I could. But if all you want is to upgrade your electrical system on board without too much studying, the sources are limited. And that is the very reason for this book, in which I have tried to keep theory to a minimum and focus on demonstrating how to carry out all the different projects.

LESSON 1: KNOW YOUR LIMITATIONS

Compared to the engine replacement that I had already completed, I found the electrical system a bit trickier – mainly because there are several different methods, and different experts promote their method (and sometimes totally condemn others).

This meant that, one way or another, I had to make a choice, without being completely certain that I had really gone for the right approach...

Naturally I made a few mistakes, but in most cases they could be put right. Alas, a short circuit during one stage of connecting up led to the demise of an expensive digital plotter. That taught me to disconnect all power when working on the system and to double-check that all cables are connected correctly (this is easier if you have a multimeter). There's not much space behind the panel and it is easy to knock into something.

LESSON 2: GET HELP WHEN YOU NEED IT

I found that the biggest disadvantage of having only limited subject expertise is that it makes it hard to plan the project before getting started – where to put things, how many and what size cables to run to different areas of the boat, etc. I did gain this knowledge, but not until the end of the (first) project.

If you have a friend with the right expertise, do ask for advice and tips on how to go about it. It may also be worthwhile to bring in a 'proper' boat electrician for certain, particularly tricky jobs, or perhaps to plan the project beforehand, something you can then follow.

LESSON 3: INVEST IN GOOD-QUALITY EQUIPMENT

Finding good-quality gear also proved difficult. My usual chandler was not much help in that respect, since they have opted for cheap instead of quality products.

Without having the right knowledge it is hard to find what you need, because you do not know how to interpret the catalogues/websites. I did get help with this from a friend who works with electronics.

Cable connectors. Finding the connectors was not easy. I bought cheap kits with a weak crimping tool from the chandler. The result was pretty poor. I had more success using connectors with shrink-type plastic and hot-melt adhesive for completely waterproof seals and protection for the exposed cable ends.

Heat-shrink tubing. It is best to try to find both black and red in suitable sizes. A heat gun is by far the easiest way to shrink the tubing. Using a naked flame is much more difficult and the result is uneven or even scorched. The tubing comes in different qualities and I would suggest you opt for a good one. If it's lined with hot-melt adhesive, so much the better.

Lights. I fitted a mixture of halogen and LEDs. The latter use significantly less power and are the first choice, but they still cost a lot more, even though prices are coming down rapidly. LED lights are the future.

Labelling. I tested several methods, including felt-tip pen on pieces of yellow plastic, which I attached with cable ties, but a labelling machine proved easier, even though that made the price per label high. The machine from Dymo was easy to use and fairly cheap; however, extra packs of plastic labels/strips were expensive.

Running cables. Running cables through flexible electrical conduits was not easy, due to the uneven internal surface. Eventually I pulled the cables through the conduits first and then fixed them in place in the boat. This meant a lot of measuring and testing before it was satisfactory. A good technique for bundling cables is important.

Good tools. Proper cable clip pliers with a release block, sharp cutting pliers or a cable-stripping tool are worth every penny.

Vaseline. Smearing Vaseline on all joints can prevent corrosion for many years. A simple, cheap and effective method.

Control panel. I made my own panel. It turned out well, although the bundled cable ties took up a lot of space, especially in front of the automatic circuit breakers when opening the hatch.

But in order to have room for the various consumer cables behind the control panel, I had to make some changes to fit the panel further forward for more space. Not a difficult job, but better planning would have helped.

Batteries. I chose AGM batteries because they have the qualities I wanted, such as withstanding many deep discharges, and a low self-discharge when you are not on the boat.

I think that for an ordinary leisure boat in UK waters, standard leisure batteries may prove more economical, even though they need to be replaced more often. They are definitely better if you are not interested in maintaining (expensive) batteries on board in almost perfect condition.

LESSON 4: BUY ONLY WHAT YOU NEED

I was not quite sure exactly how much of everything I would need, so sometimes I bought too much and sometimes (more often) too little. This meant that several times during the project I had to rush off to get something that was missing.

Now that the project is more or less completed, I have a big bag full of extra accessories that I have not used yet, but are on *Roobarb* 'just in case'. In fact, the bag has actually come in handy quite often, as I seem constantly to be adding equipment that needs power (having said that, I do test boating equipment for a living and may not be the average boat owner...).

The rest I will have to sell on the internet, or use for the next project boat – which, incidentally, is just under way. I call the new project 'From Beast to Beauty'.

Right: LED lights are now common and not very expensive. Can save a lot of energy on lights that may need to be turned on for long periods, such as nav lights

Below: A battery meter may be wise, but do not go over the top and buy the top-of-line as you may find that you will not use all features, as I did.

Above: During rewiring there were a lot of cables and equipment going in at the same time. Being very tidy will make life much easier.

Left: A no-name brand ratchet crimping tool for a perfect crimp is now so cheap there is no reason to opt for lesser quality. Easy to use for a beginner.

Right:The shrink terminals that had some melt glue inside of them were really easy to crimp and shrink to a watertight connection.

Below: If you intend to cruise the oceans, I would strongly suggest using good quality tinned cables.

Above: I have already started my next renovation, and this time I am putting in a 48/24 V electric motor in a 27 foot classic daysailer, that will have a gaff rig. But this may be for the next book ...

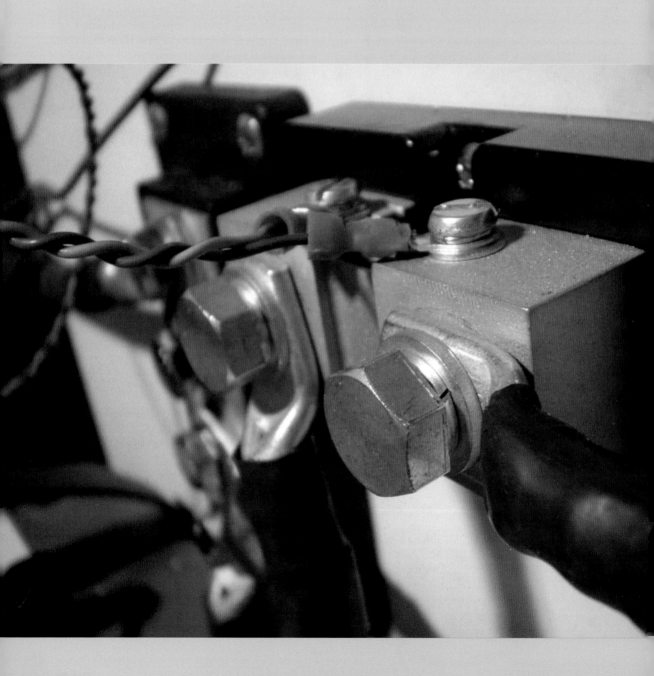

14
BASIC THEORY

BASIC THEORY

This book is not about the theory of electrical systems – it is simply about what you 'need to know' in order to update an old one. But even so, a book on boat electricity is perhaps not complete without some basic information on how it all fits together.

When I first started to carry out research for upgrading my own boat *Roobarb*, I was not particularly keen to read a lot of theory – I just wanted to dig in and fix it. I did get a couple of books but was quite disappointed because they did not tell me how to do it. Just a lot of diagrams and calculations – and this was not what I was looking for when I was ready to start the renovation of my boat.

In earlier chapters in this book, I have outlined the fundamental methods for calculating the power consumption and what diameter of cable you will need to minimise loss. I also included hints on when and how to use a multimeter.

Now let's see what is behind all this – I'll keep it short!

THE SCIENTIFIC DEFINITION MADE SIMPLE
Electricity is created when negatively charged electrons flow from one atom to the next. The centre (nucleus) of every atom is surrounded by a cloud of negatively charged particles (electrons) and positively charged particles (protons). Electricity is generated when electrons flow in a common direction in the material, and the motion is what we call electrical current.

Electrical current is a form of energy. A sufficiently strong current can be put to work: it can power motors, heating elements and hot plates, light bulbs, a TV, a computer, a microwave oven...

CURRENT
The current is measured in amperes (A, or sometimes 'amps'). Smaller currents are normally measured in milliamperes ('milliamps') (a thousandth of an ampere, or 0.001 A)

VOLTAGE
A Volt (V) is the unit used to indicate electrical potential, electrical potential difference, and electro-motive force.

The voltage on board is normally 12 or sometimes 24 V. The capacity of the battery is a little larger and nominally, and for the sake of calculations, it's 12.75 V.

RESISTANCE
Any obstruction to the flow of the current is called resistance. The resistance is measured in Ohms (Ω).

The relationship between voltage, current and resistance is defined by Ohm's Law.

Example: All copper cables have some internal resistance that hinders the flow of current. If the cable is corroded, resistance is greater.

The bigger the diameter of the cable, the easier it is for the electrons (current) to flow.

POWER

The power is the rate at which electrical energy is delivered in a circuit. It is measured in Watts (W) which equal one joule per second. It is related to the voltage and the current and can be calculated.

CALCULATIONS

To calculate the power, you multiply volts by amps to give power in Watts. If you know the wattage of the component and the battery voltage (nominally 12.75 V), you divide the wattage (W) by the voltage (V) to get the amperage (A). To calculate resistance in a cable, the formula is:

Resistance (voltage drop) = 172 x length (metres) x current (A) / area of cable (mm^2)

SAFETY

A fully charged battery will contain the current stated on the battery – say 100 A. But if short-circuited (for instance, by a spanner dropped between the terminals), the current can momentarily be so high it can start a fire or explode, which may cause battery acid to damage equipment or injure crew.

Make sure the battery isolators are turned off before you start working on the system. Use fuses for all equipment.

Shore power is potentially lethal – if you're not sure what to do, don't try to install it yourself. Get a Plug and Play shore power system – it may be a bit more expensive, but is (almost) foolproof and will also save a lot of time in the installation.

The water analogy

It is common to compare volts and amps with flowing water. It's not a very good analogy as electricity and water do not work the same way at all. However, it helps to give at least a sense of how electricity works – as long as you are not an engineer (they tend not to like this analogy!).

Imagine a water tank in the attic, which in this analogy represents a battery. When filling the tank, you are charging the battery. The height of the tank is the voltage and the flow rate (litres per minute) is the amperage.

When a tap is opened, the water will start to flow. A small diameter pipe and tap will give a feeble flow, whereas a large tap will release a plentiful flow. Here, the analogy is with cables – larger diameter cables have less resistance.

When two or more taps of equal size are open at the same time, the flow will also be small, since they share the same water tank. This is equivalent to more than one item of equipment being connected to the same cable and used at the same time. A tap giving 1 litre per hour and another tap giving 3 litres per hour gives a total consumption of 4 litres per hour.

There are books that dwell a lot more on this water analogy, if you find it intriguing...

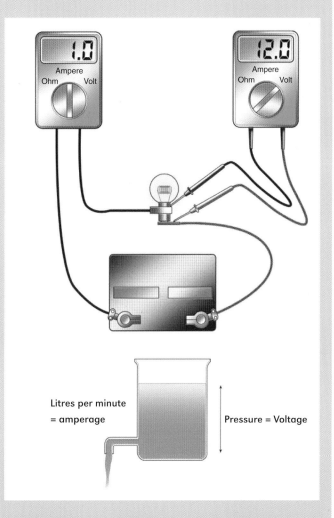

The tank represents the battery bank, and the water pressure within that tank represents voltage. The higher the water pressure (voltage), the faster the water flow (current). The more water you use, the faster the tank will empty; in the same way, the higher the voltage, the higher the current (amperage). You can also use the plumbing and pipes in this analogy to understand cable sizing – a narrow pipe will only allow a limited amount of water to flow through it. Big 'pipes' are for big consumers.

15
GLOSSARY

AC-DC AC stands for alternating current (so-called 220 V, normally 230–240 V), and DC stands for direct current and is continuous voltage (so called 12 V, normally 12.5–13.5 V).

Ampere is the unit for electrical current.

Ampere-hour (Ah) is the current flow of amps per hour.

AWG (American wire gauge) Invented in 1857 by J.R. Brown and also known as the Brown & Sharp gauge, this is the system for cable gauging in the US. The lower the number, the greater the area.

6/0 AWG	=	170.3 mm^2
5/0 AWG	=	135.1 mm^2
4/0 AWG	=	107.2 mm^2
3/0 AWG	=	85.0 mm^2
2/0 AWG	=	67.25 mm^2
0 AWG	=	53.4 mm^2
1 AWG	=	42.4 mm^2
2 AWG	=	33.6 mm^2
4 AWG	=	21.1 mm^2
6 AWG	=	13.3 mm^2
8 AWG	=	8.2 mm^2
10 AWG	=	5.3 mm^2
12 AWG	=	3.3 mm^2
13 AWG	=	2.6 mm^2
14 AWG	=	2.0 mm^2
16 AWG	=	1.3 mm^2

etc ...

Battery A battery contains a series of connected cells, which produce power through a chemical process. One cell consists of a positive electrode, an intermediate electrolyte (often absorbed in a porous separator) and a negative electrode. Strictly speaking this is an accumulator, because it can be recharged.

Black and red All cables should follow the standard colouring, not just for your sake, but for a tradesman or an eventual buyer of your boat, who should be able to work on your system.

Cable terminals Red, blue or yellow colour marks indicate the cable size that the cable clip is designed for. Red is for up to 1.5 mm^2, blue for 1.5–2.5 mm^2 and yellow for 2.6–6.0 mm^2.

Charger Steps down the 230 volts AC shore power to 12–15 volts DC through a transformer and diodes to charge a depleated battery bank up to its capacity.

Charge cycles i.e. the number of times a battery can withstand being recharged, ranging from 50 for a storage battery to several hundred for the more expensive batteries. The more a battery is discharged before recharging, the fewer cycles it can take – could be 200 cycles at 100 per cent discharge, for example, but 900 cycles at 30 per cent discharge.

Circuit breaker (CB) A mechanical switching device to protect from short circuit or overload in the AC system.

Consumer battery is the bank that usually has the largest number of batteries and supplies all the boat's daily consumers, such as the refrigerator, lighting, lamps, etc.

Converter turns one continuous voltage into another, for example 24 volt to 12 volt, or can receive 9–15 V and provide consistent 12 V output voltage. Some converters available let you choose the output voltage, for example 15/16/18/19 or 24 volt. These are perfect for running a laptop with minimal loss, rather than convert the 12 V in the battery into 240 V and then back to 14–19 V, which most laptops use.

Deep discharge is when the battery has been emptied by 50–80 per cent of its total capacity. A lead-acid battery will survive considerably longer if not discharged to more than about 30 per cent of its capacity.

EN ISO 13297 This International Standard specifies the requirements for the design, construction and installation of low-voltage AC electrical systems that operate at nominal voltages of less than 250 V single phase on small craft of hull length up to 24 m.

Float charge is a charging voltage just enough to keep the batteries at full charge without overcharging.

Fuel cell A process converts the chemical energy from a fuel (normally methanol) into electricity through a chemical reaction with oxygen, the emissions are carbon dioxide and water. The efficiency of a fuel cell is in general between 40-60 %. Fuel cells are becoming more popular and can keep the load on the batteries small or charge them overnight.

Fuse Protects the equipment and cable when a short circuit happens. There is a rule of thumb for how big a fuse should be for a certain cable. If you oversize the cable, which can be good, the fuse must be chosen according to max amperage

1.5 mm^2	10 A
2.5 mm^2	16 A
4 mm^2	20 A
6 mm^2	25 A
10 mm^2	35 A
16 mm^2	54 A
25 mm^2	70 A
35 mm^2	100 A
50 mm^2	150 A

Galvanic corrosion An electrochemical process in which one metal corrodes preferentially to another when both metals are in electrical contact and immersed in an electrolyte.

Ground, or earth In AC-powered equipment, exposed metal parts are connected to earth to prevent contact with a dangerous voltage if electrical insulation fails.

Halogen-free cable This is a requirement from the classification agencies (e.g. Lloyd's, Norske Veritas) for commercial vessels. PVC (containing halogen chloride) generates corrosive gas in a fire, which together with water creates a mist of hydrochloric acid. For a leisure boat a halogen-free cable is less important and far more expensive.

Heat resistance Cables have a heat resistance rating, usually 70°C for single cables and 90°C for high-quality cables. This represents the temperature that the copper wire inside the cable can withstand, not the ambient temperature in the engine space, for example.

Hertz A frequency of one cycle per second.

Inverter Electronically transforms 12 V DC to 240 V AC, for powering equipment that cannot be run on 12 V. In simple terms, you could say it works like an inverse battery charger.

Isolation transformer Keep the primary AC current (shore power) separated from the secondary (boat's 230 V) by magnetically transferring the current. Sometimes referred to as 'insulated' and is a safe method of not bringing earth ground on board to reduce galvanic corrosion and related problems.

Multi-wire cable The more wires, the more flexible the cable. The thicker the cable, the more important the flexibility for easy installation in the boat.

Open batteries are the commonest type of boat batteries, especially storage batteries. They should be maintained (filled with battery water), cannot withstand being tilted too much, and can produce dangerous oxyhydrogen gas if overcharged.

Parallel connection is when more than one battery is joined together to achieve a higher capacity with a sustainable current in a consumer bank. Use batteries of the same make, model and age, because discrepancies can discharge the batteries. Batteries connected in parallel have their terminals linked positive to positive and negative to negative.

The Peukert coefficient ('k') describes the decreased capacity available in a lead–acid battery the higher the rate at which it is discharged. The battery will become flatter the more amperes you take out – thus a 5 A rate for 10 hours is better for the battery than a 50 A load for one hour. The Peukert coefficient varies according to the age of the battery, generally increasing with age.

Polarity The (+) or (-) of a voltage.

Residual Current Device (RCD) Also called a ground-fault circuit interrupter. Electromechanical switching device, designed to break currents when the residual current attains a given value under specified conditions.

Ripple is the small unwanted residual periodic variation in a DC voltage, which in an inverter, for example, has been affected by the alternating waveform of AC voltage.

Sacrificial anode An electropositive metal, most commonly zinc, connected to form a galvanic cell that protects a (more important) electronegative metal from corrosion.

Self-discharge is when the battery loses its current in storage or without recharging, by 1–15 per cent per month. Some batteries (e.g. AGM) can be stored for up to a year without recharging.

Short circuit When an electrical circuit allows a current to flow along an unintended path with little or no resistance. Can cause big damage to any electrical system and equipment.

Soldering A soldered connection can sometimes cause problems and be more brittle. A connector is easier for the novice to make successfully.

Sulphating is when lead sulphate is formed on both the positive and negative electrode through absorption of the sulphuric acid in the electrolyte. Some modern battery chargers have a reconditioning mode, where higher charging voltages make the batteries 'gas', and thus release the sulphate.

Tin-plated cable Tin-plating is the process of adding a fine coating of tin (silver in aircraft), which protects the exposed copper against the oxidation that occurs in damp environments.

Trickle charge a continuous low-current charge.

Valve regulation (valve regulated lead acid battery, VRLA) means that it is a sealed system. Therefore the batteries can be placed upside down, if you wish. They do not need and cannot be filled with distilled water, but in case of heavy overcharge, there is often a relief valve that lets out gas.

Winter storage A fully charged lead-acid battery can tolerate -65°C and therefore be left in the boat over winter, possibly charging once or twice during that time. A completely empty battery can tolerate -10°C before it is destroyed by the cold.

Zinc saver Also known as a galvanic isolator. A solution to give better, even if not total, protection against stray currents that will cause galvanic corrosion. Installed in series with the AC shore-power cable to block low-voltage DC galvanic current flow. Cheaper than an isolation transformer and hence more popular.

>> INDEX

Other titles in the Adlard Coles Manuals series:

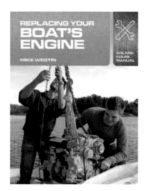

Replacing your Boat's Engine
978-1-4081-3294-4

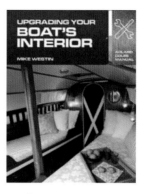

Upgrading your Boat's Interior
978-1-4081-3295-1

Other titles of interest from Adlard Coles Nautical

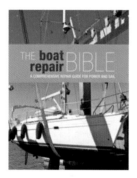

The Boat Repair Bible
978-1-4081-3321-7

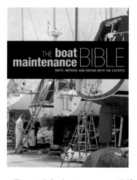

The Boat Maintenance Bible
978-1-4081-3321-7

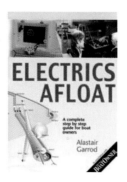

Practical Boat Owner's Electrics Afloat
978-0-7136-6149-1

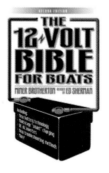

12-Volt Bible for Boats
978-0-7136-6703-5